Barry Day

THE WORLD OF
RAYMOND CHANDLER

Barry Day was born in England and received his
M.A. from Balliol College, Oxford. Day has written
about Dorothy Parker, Oscar Wilde, Johnny Mercer,
P. G. Wodehouse, and Rodgers and Hart. He has
also written and produced plays and musical revues
showcasing the work of Noël Coward, the Lunts,
Oscar Wilde, and others. Day is a Fellow of the Royal
Society of Arts and a Trustee of the Noël Coward
Foundation, and was awarded the Order of the Brit-
ish Empire by Queen Elizabeth for services to British
culture in the United States. He lives in New York,
London, and Palm Beach.

ALSO BY BARRY DAY

My Life with Noël Coward
(with Graham Payn)

Noël Coward: The Complete Lyrics

Noël Coward: In His Own Words

Noël Coward: Complete Sketches and Parodies

Theatrical Companion to Coward
(with Sheridan Morley)

The Unknown Noël:
New Writing from the Coward Archives

Coward on Film: The Cinema of Noël Coward

The Letters of Noël Coward

The Noël Coward Reader

The Complete Verse of Noël Coward

Star Quality: The Treasures of Noël Coward

This Wooden "O": Shakespeare's Globe Reborn

Oscar Wilde: A Life in Quotes

P. G. Wodehouse: In His Own Words

P. G. Wodehouse: The Complete Lyrics

Johnny Mercer: The Complete Lyrics
(with Robert Kimball)

Dorothy Parker: In Her Own Words

Sherlock Holmes: In His Own Words and
the Words of Those Who Knew Him

Sherlock Holmes and the Shakespeare Globe Murders

Sherlock Holmes and the Alice in Wonderland Murders

Sherlock Holmes and the Copycat Murders

Sherlock Holmes and the Apocalypse Murders

Sherlock Holmes and the Seven Deadly Sins Murders

Murder, My Dear Watson
(contributor)

THE WORLD OF
RAYMOND CHANDLER

THE WORLD OF
RAYMOND CHANDLER

In His Own Words

Edited by Barry Day

VINTAGE BOOKS
A Division of Penguin Random House LLC
New York

Dedicated to the man who brought magic to the mean streets

And to Lynne (who makes magic on a daily basis)

FIRST VINTAGE BOOKS EDITION, NOVEMBER 2015

Copyright © 2014 by Barry Day

All rights reserved. Published in the United States by Vintage Books, a division of Penguin Random House LLC, New York, and distributed in Canada by Random House of Canada, a division of Penguin Random House Canada Ltd., Toronto. Originally published in hardcover by Alfred A. Knopf, a division of Penguin Random House LLC, New York, in 2014.

Vintage and colophon are registered trademarks of Penguin Random House LLC.

The Library of Congress has cataloged the Knopf edition as follows
Chandler, Raymond, 1888–1959.
The world of Raymond Chandler : in his own words / edited by Barry Day.
pages   cm
1. Chandler, Raymond, 1888–1959.   2. Authors, America—20th century—Biography.
3. Detective and mystery stories—Authorship.
I. Day, Barry, editor of compilation.   II. Title
PS3505.H3224 Z46 2014
813'.52—dc23
[B] 2014009321

Anchor Books Trade Paperback ISBN: 978-0-8041-7048-2
eBook ISBN: 978-0-385-35237-6

Book design by Cassandra J. Pappas

www.vintagebooks.com

146122990

Contents

Illustrations   *ix*

Chronology   *xiii*

Introduction   *xix*

One   A MAN WITH NO HOME   3

Two   WRITING (1) Turning Pulp into Gold   19

Three   PHILIP MARLOWE Investigations   41

Four   COPS . . . AND CRIME   85

Five   THE CITY OF THE ANGELS   100

Six   HOLLYWOOD   125

Seven   DAMES . . . THE LITTLE SISTERS   163

Eight   WRITING (2) Making Magic   193

Nine   ENVOI A Long Goodbye . . . to the Big Sleep   227

Permissions and Thanks   241

Index   243

Illustrations

page:

xiv Chandler switches from *Black Mask* to *Dime Detective*

xv *Trouble Is My Business* cover

4 Raymond Chandler in Los Angeles, 1940

5 Chandler, 1890

5 Florence Thornton Chandler

6 Chandler, c. 1896

7 Front view of Dulwich College

7 Aerial view of Dulwich College

8 Chandler as a student at Dulwich

8 Chandler's Dulwich College class, 1903

9 Chandler, 1905

10 Chandler, 1906

12 Chandler in Gordon Highlander uniform

13 Chandler, 1918, British Columbia Regiment

14 Chandler, 1918, R.A.F.

15 Chandler after the war

15 With his mother at Cypress Grove, California

16 Chandler, 1920s

17 Cissy Pascal

19 Cissy as an artist's model

21 The Chandlers' marriage license

22 The Accounting Department of the Dabney Oil Syndicate, 1920

22 *Black Mask* illustration

23 *Black Mask* cover

24 The *Black Mask* gang

26 Dashiell Hammett

28 James M. Cain

29 Erle Stanley Gardner

30 Ernest Hemingway

33 F. Scott and Zelda Fitzgerald

34 W. Somerset Maugham

35 Eugene O'Neill

38 Alfred A. Knopf

38 Blanche Knopf

39 *The Big Sleep* jacket, 1939

42 Lauren Bacall and Humphrey Bogart in *The Big Sleep*, 1946

44 Greystone Mansion

45 *The Big Sleep,* Hamish Hamilton, 1939

45 *The Lady in the Lake*, Hamish Hamilton, 1944

46 Chandler, 1939

50 Audrey Totter and Robert Montgomery in *La Dame du Lac*, 1946

52 Robert Montgomery as Philip Marlowe

53 The Dionne Quintuplets

54 Camel cigarettes

56 Marlowe's "assistants": the Luger P08, Colt .38, and Smith &
    Wesson .38

56 Marmon 34 Touring Car, Oldsmobile Series 60, 1937 Chrysler
    Airflow

58 Marlowe's apartment building on Hightower Drive

61 Old Forester scotch

61 Huggins-Young coffee

64 Jacket for *The Little Sister*

85 LAPD badge

87 Prohibition—the Volstead Act

91 Police cruiser, c. 1950

100 Los Angeles at night

101 Ross Macdonald

102 Los Angeles at night

103 Grauman's Chinese Theatre

104 The house in which Joe Brody was murdered in *The Big Sleep*

104 Wilshire Boulevard, 1935

105 Hollywood Boulevard, 1937

106 Brown Derby restaurant

107 Vine Street, 1953

108 City Hall and Union Station

110 The Beverly Hills Hotel

112 Richfield Building, 1955

113 Bunker Hill

117 Art deco Sunset Tower

119 Bay City

121 Chandler's house at 6005 Camino de la Costa, La Jolla, California

122 The smog of Los Angeles

125 Hollywoodland sign

128 The Bronson Gate at Paramount

129 Chandler chats with Fred MacMurray

129 Chandler and Billy Wilder, 1943

130 Phyllis Dietrichson and Walter Neff, *Double Indemnity*, 1944

132 Letter to James M. Cain from Chandler

133 Cain's reply

134 Walter Neff in the death chamber

141 Veronica Lake as Joyce Harwood in *The Blue Dahlia*

141 Lake with Alan Ladd on the movie poster for *The Blue Dahlia*

142 John Houseman

143 Chandler in 1945

148 Paul Henreid lights up Bette Davis in Warner Bros.' 1942 *Now, Voyager*

150 Schwab's Pharmacy on Sunset and Crescent Heights

152 Dick Powell plays Marlowe opposite Claire Trevor in *Murder, My Sweet*, 1944

154 Howard Hawks

155 *The Lady in the Lake,* 1946

158 Farley Granger and Robert Walker, *Strangers on a Train*, 1951

164 Veronica Lake

165 Lauren Bacall as Vivian Regan in *The Big Sleep*, 1946

169 Audrey Totter as Adrienne Fromsett in *The Lady in the Lake*

173 Martha Vickers as Carmen Sternwood in *The Big Sleep*

174 Claire Trevor as Mrs. Grayle/Velma

178 Nancy Guild as Merle Davis in *The Brashear Doubloon*

182 Nina Van Pallandt as Eileen Wade in *The Long Goodbye*

186 The mature Taki with the mature Chandler, mid-1930s

188 Ray and Taki at work in La Jolla, c. 1948

190 April 9, 1948

191 Taki as a kitten, 1932

196 *The Simple Art of Murder* jacket

197 *The Simple Art of Murder* hardcover

199 Chandler's corrections for a draft of his sixth novel

224 Dame Agatha Christie

225 One of the many foreign-language editions

230 *The Long Goodbye*

232 Helga Greene

233 Natasha Spender

236 Foreign editions of Chandler's books

238 Chandler shortly before his death, 1959

239 Angel's Flight, Bunker Hill, 1956, by William Reagh

Chronology

1888 Raymond Thornton Chandler born July 23 in Chicago.

1895 Chandler's parents divorce. His mother takes him to London.

1900 He attends Dulwich College, a traditional English public school.

1905 Leaves school and goes to Paris to study French, and later to Munich.

1907 He returns to England and becomes a naturalized British subject. He then passes the Civil Service exam with distinction and goes to work for the Admiralty.

1908 After a few months he decides to leave and become a writer.

1909–1911 Works as a reporter and occasionally contributes pieces to *The Westminster Gazette* and *The Academy.*

1912 He returns to America, travels around and finds himself in Los Angeles, where he moves from one job to another.

1917 He enlists in the Canadian Expeditionary Force and goes back to England.

1918 Serves at the front in France for three months before being transferred to the Royal Air Force.

1919 He is discharged now that the war is over and returns to the West Coast.

Begins an affair with Cissy Pascal, a married woman eighteen years his senior.

1920 Cissy divorces her husband but she and Chandler delay their own marriage because his mother disapproves, due to the age disparity.

1922 Chandler takes a clerical job with the Dabney Oil Syndicate, where he will eventually rise to the position of vice president.

1924 His mother dies and he marries Cissy.

1925–1931 The couple moves restlessly around the Los Angeles area and Chandler begins to drink heavily.

1932 He is fired from Dabney as a result of his drinking.

Decides to concentrate on his writing and begins to work in the area of "pulp."

1933 His first story, "Blackmailers Don't Shoot," is published in the magazine *Black Mask.* Chandler is now forty-five.

1934 "Smart Aleck Kill" and "Finger Man" follow in *Black Mask.*

1935 "Killer in the Rain," "Nevada Gas" and "Spanish Blood."

1936 "Guns at Cyrano's," "The Man Who Liked Dogs," "Goldfish," "The Curtain" and "Try the Girl."

1937 . . . and Chandler switches from Black Mask *to* Dime Detective *and publishes "Mandarin's Jade."*

Trouble Is My Business *began life as a "John Dalmas" story in* Dime Detective. *By the time it appeared in book form, John Dalmas was Philip Marlowe.*

1938 "Red Wind," "The King in Yellow" and "Bay City Blues."

He begins writing his first novel, *The Big Sleep,* using reworked elements from some of the earlier stories. In doing so, he creates the character Philip Marlowe. The job takes him three months.

1939 *The Big Sleep* is published by Alfred A. Knopf.

"Pearls Are a Nuisance" and "Trouble Is My Business" are published in *Dime Detective.*

"I'll Be Waiting" is published in *The Saturday Evening Post.*

The Chandlers move to La Jolla, California.

1940 The peripatetic couple moves to Monrovia and then to Arcadia.

Farewell, My Lovely is published by Knopf.

From Arcadia, the Chandlers move to Santa Monica, which becomes "Bay City" in Chandlerworld.

1941 RKO pays Chandler $2,000 for the movie rights to *Farewell, My Lovely.* (The first version, *The Falcon Takes Over*—part of an ongoing "B" series—is released the following year; the second, *Murder, My Sweet,* in 1944.)

1942   Chandler finishes *The High Window* and sells the movie rights to 20th Century Fox for $3,500. (The first version, *Time to Kill*, is released in 1943; the second version, *The Brasher Doubloon*, in 1947.)

      The High Window is published by Knopf.

1943   Chandler signs with Paramount to work on the screenplay of James M. Cain's *Double Indemnity* with director Billy Wilder. He is paid $1,750 a week—a far cry from the one cent per word he received from *Black Mask*.

      The Lady in the Lake is published by Knopf.

      His essay "The Simple Art of Murder" is published in *The Atlantic Monthly*.

1944   *Double Indemnity* is released and becomes a considerable success.

      Chandler is nominated for an Oscar for his screenplay.

1945   He continues writing for Paramount but *The Blue Dahlia* is the only other project to achieve success.

      MGM signs him to work on the screenplay of *The Lady in the Lake,* but he is dissatisfied with the way the film is developing and leaves before the work is finished, insisting that his name be removed from the credits.

1946   *The Blue Dahlia* is released and Chandler is again nominated for an Academy Award for the screenplay.

      Warner Bros. releases *The Big Sleep*.

      The Chandlers return to La Jolla.

1948   Chandler leaves Knopf for Houghton Mifflin.

1949   *The Little Sister* is published.

1950   Chandler begins work with Alfred Hitchcock on *Strangers on a Train* at Warner Bros., but the two men don't get along and Chandler is replaced.

1951   Chandler begins writing *The Long Goodbye.*

1952   The Chandlers make an extended stay in England.

      Chandler's health is beginning to deteriorate.

1953   *The Long Goodbye* is published by Houghton Mifflin.

1954   Cissy Chandler dies. Chandler goes into deep mourning and alcohol-fueled depression.

1955   He sells the La Jolla home and moves to London.

1956 Returns to the U.S., being now a tax exile from the U.K.

1957 In New York he is hospitalized because of his heavy drinking.

He finishes *Playback*.

1958 London again . . . and hospital again.

Playback published.

One more return to La Jolla . . . and several more returns to the hospital.

1959 Chandler proposes marriage to his agent, Helga Greene. She accepts but her father's antipathy sends Chandler into the final spiral of depression.

He returns to New York to accept the presidency of Mystery Writers of America.

Shortly afterward, in La Jolla, he contracts pneumonia and dies in the Scripps Clinic there.

Chandler is buried in the Mount Hope Cemetery in San Diego, sleeping The Big Sleep.

Introduction

I'm just a fellow who jacked up a few pulp novelettes into book form . . . All I'm looking for is an excuse for certain experiments in dramatic dialogue. To justify them I have to have plot and situation; but fundamentally I care almost nothing about either. All I really care about is what Errol Flynn calls "the music," the lines he has to speak.

> Letter to Frederick Lewis Allen—May 7, 1948

A writer who hates the actual writing, who gets no joy out of the creation of magic by words, to me is simply not a writer at all . . . How can you hate the magic which makes a paragraph or sentence or a line of dialogue or a description something in the nature of a new creation?

> Letter to Hamish Hamilton—September 19, 1951

===

This is not another biography of Raymond Chandler—or only incidentally.

The salient facts of his life are by now well known to any Chandler enthusiast. Ricocheting in his early years between small-town America and an English public (private) school, carefully observing both cultures but feeling he really belonged to neither, he remained "a man with no home," as he described himself in later life.

Nonetheless, the experience developed in him a sense of objectivity as he learned the true meaning of "divided by a common language."

Words fascinated him from the first, and his "classical" education in Latin and Greek made him value them for their precise meaning. Only then could you play with them knowingly, as he did when he came to write his "pulp" stories and had to learn a new language called "American."

As his skill developed and he became—along with Dashiell Hammett—one of the doyens of "hard-boiled fiction," it wasn't his plots or supporting characters that set him apart. It was his use of language. He was simply the most literate in his league, and he had little patience with contemporaries—such as James M. Cain and even Hemingway—who, in his view, were lazy with language.

He was the master of the exaggerated simile—"I think I rather invented the trick," he once said. And even when he later admitted that he sometimes took the trick too far—"I did run them into the ground"—the words still sang on the page. He was happy to yield the palm to the Agatha Christies and Rex Stouts when it came to ingenuity of construction, but "their words don't get up and walk—mine do!"

It seems appropriate, then, to take Chandler at his own words. To let him, through quotation and with a little linkage here and there, analyze the people and places that dominate his work . . . the Dames, the Cops, the Crooks . . . the places, like Los Angeles with its "mean streets," that become characters in themselves . . . and never forgetting a man called Marlowe.

Welcome to the World of Raymond Chandler—in the Words of Raymond Chandler . . .

BARRY DAY

2014

THE WORLD OF
RAYMOND CHANDLER

One

A Man with No Home

What is really the matter with me is that I have no home and no one to care for in a home, if I had one.

—Letter to Neil Morgan—February 20, 1956

A man who has no country will often invent his own.

Raymond Chandler did just that. American-born, raised in Edwardian England ("English manners don't intimidate me"), then voluntarily repatriated to the surrealistic frontiersville of Southern California, he took elements of what he found there and created an emotional universe out of the Los Angeles he saw that became just as much a character in his fiction as any of the people he invented to populate it.

He took pride in the fact that "I was the first to write about Southern California at all realistically" and was saddened by what he saw happening to it. The industrial smog wasn't the only form of pollution on the horizon. "Now half the writers in the country piddle around in the smog. Los Angeles is just a tired old whore to me now," he wrote in 1956. By that time he was tired himself—tired of writing and tired of life. But that was a long time and a brilliant career later . . .

The swans of our childhood were probably just pigeons.

—Raymond Chandler

Raymond Thornton Chandler was born in Chicago on July 23, 1888, of an American father, who was a civil engineer, and an Anglo-Irish mother. It was a scenario he would gladly have rewritten.

> I was conceived in Laramie, Wyoming, and if they had asked me, I should have preferred to be born there. I always liked high altitudes and Chicago is not a place where an Anglophile would choose to be born.

It was a place he was soured by quite early on. "When I was a kid in Chicago I saw a cop shoot a little white dog to death." It didn't do much to make him feel benevolent toward the law, either.

All of this—as he told his publisher, Hamish Hamilton, in 1950— "was so damned long ago that I wish I had never told anybody when. Both my parents were of Quaker descent. Neither was a practicing Quaker. My mother was born in Waterford, Ireland, my father came of a Pennsylvania farming family, probably one of the batch that settled with William Penn."

1940. Raymond Chandler in Los Angeles. Alfred A. Knopf

1890. Handwritten caption reads: "Alfred Raymond Chandler relaxing."
Bodleian Library, Oxford

Chandler's mother—Florence Thornton Chandler.

At the age of seven I had scarlet fever in a hotel, and I understand this is a very rare accomplishment. I remember principally the ice cream and the pleasure of pulling the loose skin off during convalescence.

The Chandlers moved to Nebraska . . .

I remember the oak trees and the high wooden sidewalks beside the dirt roads and the heat and the fireflies and walking sticks and a lot of strange insects . . . and the dead cattle and once in a while a dead man floating down the muddy river and the dandy little three-hole privy behind the house . . . I remember the rocking chairs on the edge of the sidewalk in a solid row outside the hotel . . .

—Letter to Charles Morton—November 20, 1944

He would remember those old hotels when he came to describe their L.A. equivalents.

c. 1896. Chandler in Waterford, Ireland. When he was a child his mother would take him to visit relatives.

When his father, Maurice, deserted them ("an utter swine"), his mother, Florence, headed home to Ireland in 1895 with young Raymond in tow. They later moved on to England and stayed with her family in the London suburb of Norwood. After the age of seven Chandler never saw his father again.

> An amazing people, the Anglo-Irish. They never mixed with Catholics socially . . . I grew up with a terrible contempt for Catholics, and I have trouble with it even now . . .
> —Letter to Charles Morton—January 1, 1945

His mother sent him to Dulwich College, a second-rank public school "not quite on a level with Eton and Harrow from a social point

Two views of Dulwich College, one of the better public schools in England, located in a London suburb. Courtesy of Dulwich College

As a student at Dulwich College.
"I don't think education ever did
me any great harm."
Bodleian Library, Oxford

1903. The Classical Lower Fifth in midsummer. Courtesy of Dulwich College

*1905. The year he went to
Paris to study French.*

of view but very good educationally." There he was a contemporary
of P. G. Wodehouse and William Henry Pratt (Boris Karloff). In
those days the school had two "sides"—the Modern Side, intended
for boys who were likely to end up in business, and the Classical Side
for those with ambitions to learn the Latin and Greek to take them
to Oxford or Cambridge. The young Chandler was bright enough to
be able to combine both sides, and it was here that he acquired the
"classical education" he would refer to proudly (and frequently) for
the rest of his life. It was quite conceivable that he could have gone on
to university but the uncle (Ernest) who was subsidizing his education
felt that enough was enough. The avuncular view was that the young
Chandler's proper destination should be the Civil Service, and that
the boy now needed some more practical qualifications.

As a result, he left school in 1905 at the age of seventeen and
embarked on a cut-down version of the traditional European "grand
tour," spending six months each in Paris and Germany. He appears—in
those days at least—to have had a facility for languages. After working with a private tutor he could speak German "well enough to be

1906. Raymond Chandler, World Traveler. On leaving Dulwich he spent six months each in Paris and here in Germany, learning the languages.

taken for a German," but the French were, predictably, a tougher nut to crack. "One never speaks well enough to satisfy a Frenchman. *Il sait se faire comprendre* is about as far as they will go" (Letter to Wesley Hartley—November 11, 1957).

On his return, the Civil Service examination loomed . . . "I wanted to be a writer, but I knew my Irish uncle would not stand for that, so I thought perhaps that the easy hours in the Civil Service might let me do that on the side. I passed third in a group of about six hundred." He was posted to the Admiralty but found the work so "stultifying" that he resigned after only six months—much to his uncle's irritation.

I thoroughly detested the civil service. I had too much Irish in my blood to stand being pushed around by suburban nobodies. I wanted to be a barrister, but I didn't have enough money.

So I holed up in Bloomsbury, lived on next to nothing, and wrote for a highbrow weekly review [*The Academy*] and also for

The Westminster Gazette . . . But at the best I made only a bare living.
　　　　—Letter to Leroy Wright—March 31, 1957

He wrote reviews, essays, satirical sketches (in emulation of Saki),
anything that occurred to him that the editors would print. ("My first
piece of writing was a poem.")

The sketches written . . . away back when I was an elegant young
thing with an Old Alleynian hatband on a very natty basket weave
straw hat . . . show childish petulance and a frustrated attempt to
be brilliant about nothing.
　　　　—Letter to Charles Morton—December 18, 1944

For all of this, he had to struggle to net more than three or four
pounds a week. He prided himself particularly on his verse, though
in retrospect, "most of which now seems to me as deplorable, but not
all." He would later describe it as "Grade B Georgian."

> Come with me, love,
> Across the world,
> Ere glory fades
> And wings are furled,
> And we will wander hand in hand,
> Like a boy and girl in a playroom land.
> —Excerpt from "A Woman's Way" in
> 　　*Westminster Gazette*—April 22, 1909

> A little twist or phrase or thought
> This way or that
> To give it an air of meaning such a lot
> More than it says.
> —Excerpt from "Free Verse"　unpublished

He later prided himself on the fact that he had never subscribed to
the "I-dare-you-not-to-understand-what-I-am-talking-about" school
of poetry. As for his early essays, they were, he felt, "of intolerable
preciousness of tone, but already quite nasty in tone."

It is possible that like Max Beerbohm, I was born half a century too late, and that I, too, belong to an age of grace.

—Letter to Alfred Knopf—January 12, 1946

After "several years freelancing in London in a rather undistin-guished way," he was forced to the regretful conclusion that the role of the amateur writer was one for those clever young men who were professionally employed—doing something else for a living.

I was distinctly not a clever young man. Nor was I at all a happy young man. I had very little money . . . I had grown up in England and all my relatives were either English or Colonial. And yet I was not English. I had no feeling of identity with the United States, and yet I resented the kind of snobbish criticism of the Americans that was current at that time.

"A Gordon for me, a Gordon for me,/If ye're no a Gordon, ye're no use to me,/The Black Watch are braw, the Seaforth and a'/But the cocky wee Gordon's the pride o' them 'a.' "
—*Traditional Scottish song*

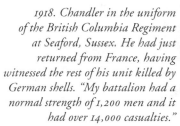

1918. Chandler in the uniform of the British Columbia Regiment at Seaford, Sussex. He had just returned from France, having witnessed the rest of his unit killed by German shells. "My battalion had a normal strength of 1,200 men and it had over 14,000 casualties."

While he was studying in Paris he had run into a number of Americans,

> and most of them seemed to have a lot of bounce and liveliness and to be thoroughly enjoying themselves in situations where the average Englishman of the same class would be stuffy or completely bored. But I wasn't one of them. I didn't even speak their language. I was, in effect, a man without a country . . .
> —Letter to Hamish Hamilton—December 11, 1950

Years later he would echo Shaw's line:

> There can be no greater mistake than to think that we and the English people speak the same language.
> —Letter to Neil Morgan—June 3, 1955

In 1912 at the age of twenty-four he took the plunge and immigrated to the United States with a £500 loan "from my irate uncle (every penny of it was repaid with six per cent interest)."

Then came the "Great War"—the "war to end all wars"—and Chandler enlisted in the Canadian Gordon Highlanders. He served in France and rose to the rank of sergeant and then platoon commander . . .

> Courage is a strange thing: One can never be sure of it . . . If you had to go over the top somehow all you seemed to think of was trying to keep the men spaced, in order to reduce casualties.
> —Letter to Deidre Gartrell—March 2, 1957

> Once you have had to lead a platoon into direct machine-gun fire, nothing is ever the same again.

Most of the men were in fact killed in action, and the survivors, including Chandler, were sent back to England and transferred to the Royal Air Force. Before he had time to complete his flight training

1918. Chandler was transferred from the Canadian army to the R.A.F. Bodleian Library, Oxford

*Chandler back in
California after the war.*

the Armistice was signed and he was demobilized. He and his mother
returned to America.

In those early years there he had such a variety of jobs that he
might have been suspected of collecting them for the cover of the
eventual paperback. There is no evidence of the highly-favored lum-
berjack or short-order cook, but for the rest . . .

*Chandler and his mother at Cypress Grove, California, soon after the end of World
War I.* Bodleian Library, Oxford

I arrived in California in 1919 with a beautiful wardrobe, a public school accent, no practical gifts for earning a living, and a contempt for the natives which, I am sorry to say, has in some measure persisted to this day. I had a pretty hard time trying to make a living. Once I worked on an apricot ranch ten hours a day, twenty cents an hour. Another time I worked for a sporting goods house, stringing tennis rackets for $12.50 a week. I taught myself book-keeping and from there on my rise was as rapid as the growth of a sequoia . . .

—Letter to Hamish Hamilton—November 10, 1950

He made no secret of the fact that he detested business life but undoubtedly had an aptitude for it. The bookkeeping course that was

Chandler in the 1920s.

*Cissy Pascal
(née Pearl Eugénie Hurlburt).*
Bodleian Library, Oxford

scheduled to take three years, Chandler completed in six weeks. And when he settled on the oil business as his speciality, "I finally became an officer or director of half a dozen independent oil corporations . . . They were small companies, but very rich."

"Business is very tough and I hate it," he would write to his literary agent, Helga Greene (May 5, 1957). "But whatever you set out to do, you have to do as well as you know how . . ."

I once hoped to be a comparative philologist (just a boyhood fancy, no doubt).

"The depression finished that," but by that time he had already passed two turning points in his personal life. In 1924 his mother died. That same year in Los Angeles he married a divorcée—Pearl Eugénie Hurlburt ("Cissy") Pascal. She was an older woman and at the time they married he may not have realized just how much older she was; her birth certificate and her marriage license differ by ten years. In fact, she was then fifty-three to Chandler's thirty-five. Despite her continued ill health in later years, it was a happy marriage, "as happy a marriage as any man could expect."

"For thirty years, ten months and four days, she was the light of my life, my whole ambition," he told Hamish Hamilton. "Anything else I did was just the fire for her to warm her hands at. That is all there is to say."

That was the good news. The bad news was that he had begun to drink heavily—an expensive as well as illegal activity during Prohibition, which lasted from 1920 to 1933. It was the alcohol as much as the Depression that ended his business career. His last employer sacked him in 1932. He was then forty-four and had absolutely no idea what he was going to do to pay their bills.

"I still think of myself as an exile," he wrote to Hamish Hamilton in 1946, "and want to come back. But I suppose it will be years before that is a reasonable thing to do."

Two

Writing (1)

Turning Pulp into Gold

The young Cissy lived in New York. On occasion she worked as an artist's model. Bodleian Library, Oxford

I had to learn American just like a foreign language . . .
—Letter to Alex Barris —March 18, 1949

The chances are I'll never get written half of what there is in my mind asking to be written at this moment.
>—Letter to John Hersey—March 29, 1948

The French are the only people I know of who think about writing as writing. The Anglo-Saxons think first of the subject matter, and second, if at all, of the quality.
>—Letter to James Sandoe, January 26, 1944

Thank heaven that when I tried to write fiction I had the sense to do it in a language that was not all steamed up with rhetoric.
>—Raymond Chandler

He did not write about crime, or detection . . . He wrote about the corruption of the human Spirit.
>—George V. Higgins—1988

"You're looking at a small time operator in a small time business . . . All writers are punks and I am one of the punkest."
>—Novelist Roger Wade in *The Long Goodbye*

There is nothing to write about but death, and the detective story is a tragedy with a happy ending.
>—Letter to James Sandoe—June 2, 1949

━━━━━

When he arrived in America, Chandler was painfully realistic about his chances of literary success. His early efforts in England had not exactly set London alight. "So far I had shown very little talent for writing, and that little was riddled with intellectual snobbery."

With the distraction of having to earn a living, he published virtually nothing for more than a decade. What would he write *about* in this alien land? The answer came by apparent happenstance . . .

In 1931 my wife and I used to cruise up and down the Pacific Coast (in our automobile) in a very leisurely way, and at night, just to have something to read, I would pick a pulp magazine off a rack (because they were cheap enough to throw away and because I never had any time or any taste for the kind of thing which is known as women's magazines) . . . it struck me that some of the writing was pretty forceful and honest, even though it had its crude aspect. I decided that might be a good way to try to learn to write fiction and get paid a small amount of money at the same time.

—Letter to Hamish Hamilton—November 10, 1950

There was a distinct sameness about the content of pulp stories which—as with any form of literature— was attributable in large part to the social context.

Today we have "police procedurals," which follow—and to a degree extol—modern methods of detection. In the thirties the heroes were

1924. The Chandlers' marriage license. Cissy was actually ten years older than the date she gave. To Chandler she was "the beat of my heart for thirty years."

1920. The Accounting Department of the Dabney Oil Syndicate. Chandler is on the extreme left of the back row. Bodleian Library, Oxford

"I had to learn American just like a foreign language . . ."

Black Mask. *"It struck me that some of the writing was pretty forceful and honest."*

invariably lone private eyes, to some extent Robin Hoods, for the simple reason that the public didn't trust the police. Corruption was seen to be rife, and so a cop, by definition, couldn't be a credible hero. The genre was defined by that fact alone.

Violence in the stories was *de rigueur*—partly because the readers of the pulps had come to expect it and partly because it reflected the current reality of the Prohibition era, when armed confrontation between rival mobs was commonplace. The body count in Chandler's first story, "Blackmailers Don't Shoot," probably exceeded the sum total of all the subsequent novels.

First Chandler had to learn the language. "To learn it I had to study and analyze it. As a result, when I use slang, colloquialism, snide talk or any kind of off-beat language, I do it deliberately" (Letter to Alex Barris—March 18, 1949). "It would seem that a classical education might be rather a poor basis for writing novels in a hard-boiled

The Black Mask *Gang. The first* Black Mask *West Coast Get-Together, January 11, 1936. This dinner was the only occasion Chandler and Dashiell Hammett ever met. Left to right, seated: Arthur Barnes, John K. Butler, W. T. Ballard, Horace McCoy and Norbert Davis. Standing are Raymond T. Moffatt, Chandler, Herbert Stinson, Dwight Babcock, Eric Taylor and Hammett.* Bodleian Library, Oxford

vernacular. I happen to think otherwise. A classical education saves you from being fooled by pretentiousness, which is what most current fiction is too full of," he wrote to producer John Houseman and to Hamish Hamilton. "If I hadn't grown up with Latin and Greek, I doubt if I would know so well where to draw the very subtle line between what I call the vernacular style and what I should call an illiterate or *faux naïf* style."

He was never comfortable in the role. As late as 1950 he was telling Hamish Hamilton,

> As a mystery writer I think I am a bit of an anomaly, since most mystery writers of the American school are only semi-literate, and I am not only literate but intellectual, much as I dislike the term.

He was an apt student, as many other writers—such as Nabokov, Conrad and Stoppard—have proved to be when they learned another language in their maturity. He took five months to polish "Blackmailers Don't Shoot," an 18,000-word novella for which he received $180 from the leading pulp magazine, *Black Mask.* "This was in the great days of the *Black Mask* (if I may call them great days)," when a writer for the pulps had to produce a million words to earn $10,000.

> All I wanted to do . . . was to play with a fascinating new language, to see what it would do as a means of expression which might remain on the level of unintellectual thinking and yet acquire the power to say things which are usually only said with a literary air. I really didn't care what kind of story I wrote; I wrote melodrama because, when I looked around me, it was the only kind of writing I saw that was relatively honest.
>
> —Letter to Dale Warren—January 7, 1945

Not only was it "honest"—it had vitality,

> Even at its most mannered it made most of the fiction of the time taste like a cup of lukewarm consommé at a spinsterish tea-room.
>
> —Introduction to *Trouble Is My Business*

> [In preparing "Blackmailers"] I did something I have never been able to persuade any other writer to do . . . I made a detailed synopsis of some story—say by [Erle Stanley] Gardner . . . and then tried to write the story. Then I compared it with professional work and saw where I had failed to make an effect, or had the pace wrong, or some other mistake. Then I did it over and over again.
>
> —Letter to James Howard—March 26, 1957

"Analyze and imitate" was a credo he followed throughout his career. "Any writer who cannot teach himself cannot be taught by others."

He was greatly taken—both then and later—with the special qualities of "American English" and at one point tried to analyze it. Again, the classical education was in evidence:

It is a fluid language, like Shakespearean English, and easily takes in new words, new meanings for old words . . . It is more alive to clichés . . . its impact is sensational rather than intellectual . . . It is a mass language . . . which is being molded by writers to do delicate things and yet be within the grasp of superficially educated people.

He was critical of the way the average American appeared to undervalue it. "You hear American doctors and lawyers and school-masters talking in such a way that it is very clear they have no real understanding of their own language . . . All the best American writing has been done by men who are, or at some time were, cosmopolitans . . . but they had to have European taste to use the material."
And as for Americans in general . . .

The average "educated" American has the all round mental equipment of a fourth form boy in an English public school.

He was under no illusion that the road ahead was likely to be paved with golden kudos. Nonetheless, it was his ambition, he said, "to get

Dashiell Hammett (1884–1961).
Chandler wrote, "Hammett is
the ace performer . . . he was
spare, frugal, hard-boiled, but
he did over and over again
what only the best writers can
ever do at all. He wrote scenes
that seemed never to have been
written before . . . The gulf
between Hammett and the
merely rough boys seems to me
vast." Photofest

murder away from the upper classes, the weekend house party, and the vicar's rose garden and back to the people who are really good at it."

> In this country the mystery writer is looked down upon as sub-literary merely because he is a mystery writer rather than, for instance, a writer of social significance twaddle. To a classicist—even a very rusty one—such an attitude is merely a *parvenu* insecurity.
>
> —Letter to Hamish Hamilton—November 10, 1950

"After that ["Blackmailers"] I never looked back, although I had a good many uneasy periods looking forward," he wrote to Hamilton. In the five years that followed, he began to build a reputation in the ten-cent pulp magazines, such as *Dime Detective* and *Detective Fiction Weekly*—*Black Mask* cost an impressive fifteen cents—until he was earning $400 a story when it appeared on the cover. Even so, "Mine was, of course, a losing game. I wrote pulp stories with as much care as slick stories. It was very poor pay for the work that I put into them."

Nonetheless, he was learning his trade—and he had a lot to learn besides the nuances of this new language:

> When I started out to write fiction I had the great disadvantage of having absolutely no talent for it . . . If more than two people were on scene I couldn't keep one of them alive. A crowded canvas just bewilders me. Give me two people snotting each other across a desk and I'm happy.
>
> —Letter to Paul Brooks—1949

> I couldn't get a character in or out of a room, I couldn't even get his hat off.
>
> —Letter to Wesley Hartley—December 3, 1957

The stories would often be suggested by something he happened to read in the papers or overhear:

> I learn something too hot for the papers to publish, and it starts me thinking, and then my imagination takes over.

*James M. Cain
(1892–1977).*
Photofest

The idea of Geiger, the homosexual who runs a private pornography library in *The Big Sleep,* was supposedly inspired by such a tip.

He was also studying his established competitors—the Dashiell Hammetts, the Erle Stanley Gardners and the James M. Cains, but also the rest of the following pack. "A schoolmaster of mine long ago said—'You can only learn from the second-raters. The first-raters are out of range; you can't see how they get their effects.' There is a lot of truth in this" (Letter to Helga Greene—April 30, 1957).

Hammett was a good example. "He had style, but his audience didn't know it because it was a language not supposed to be capable of such refinements. From "The Simple Art of Murder":

Hammett took murder out of the Venetian vase and dropped it into the alley . . .

Hammett is the ace performer . . .

He was spare, frugal, hard-boiled, but he did over and over again what only the best writers can ever do at all. He wrote scenes that seemed never to have been written before.

He served the supreme purpose—Chandler claimed—of "giving the detective story back to people who commit murder for a purpose and not just to provide a corpse."

Chandler concluded early on that "the great fault of American mystery writers . . . is a lack of texture, a sort of naiveté which probably comes from them not being very well educated or well read" (Letter to Dorothy Gardner—January 1956).

He had a particular admiration for the technical expertise of the prolific Erle Stanley Gardner:

> The ability to put over situations which verged on the implausible but which in the reading seemed quite real . . . I have never come even near to doing it myself. Dumas had this quality in a very strong degree. Also Dickens. It's probably the fundamental of all rapid work, because naturally rapid work has a large measure of improvisation, and to make an improvised scene seem inevitable is quite a trick . . . And here I am writing about technique, in spite of a strong conviction that the moment a man begins to talk about technique, that's proof he's fresh out of ideas.
>
> —Letter to Erle Stanley Gardner—May 5, 1939

*Erle Stanley Gardner
(1889–1970).*
Photofest

Ernest ("Papa") Hemingway
(1898–1961).

"Who is this Hemingway person
at all?"
    "A guy that keeps saying the
same thing over and over until you
begin to believe it must be good."
—Farewell, My Lovely

I suppose the weakness, even the
tragedy, of writers like Hemingway
is that their sort of stuff demands
an immediate vitality; and a
man outgrows his vitality without
unfortunately outgrowing his
furious concern with it.
—*Letter to Charles Morton—*
    October 9, 1950
Photofest

Chandler and Gardner formed a mutual admiration society. Chandler felt Gardner "owed nothing to Hammett or Hemingway" (the ultimate compliment), while Gardner called Chandler "a star of the first magnitude."

I wish I had one of those facile plotting brains, like Erle Gardner.

Gardner was highly prolific and used to dictate his dozens of books. He was also very talkative, and it amused Chandler that "years of yapping into a Dictaphone machine have destroyed the quality of his voice, which now has all the delicate chiaroscuro of a French taxi horn."

He was prepared to admit that

Hammett is all right. I give him everything. There were a lot of things he could not do, but what he did he did superbly. But James Cain—faugh! Everything he touches smells like a billy-goat. He is every kind of writer I detest, a *faux naïf,* a Proust in greasy overalls, a dirty little boy with a piece of chalk and a board fence and nobody looking. Such people are the offal of literature, not because they write about dirty things, but because they do it in a dirty way. Nothing hard and clean and cold and ventilated. A brothel with a smell of cheap scent in the front parlor and a bucket of slops at the back door. Do I, for God's sake, sound like that?

—Letter to Blanche Knopf—October 22, 1942

From the outset he hoped the day would come "when I don't have to ride around on Hammett and James Cain, like an organ grinder's monkey."

Ironically, it was his 1943 screenplay of Cain's *Double Indemnity*—in collaboration with director Billy Wilder—that earned him the first of his Academy Award nominations.

I suppose the weakness, even the tragedy, of writers like Hemingway is that their sort of stuff demands an immense vitality; and a man outgrows his vitality without unfortunately outgrowing his furious concern with it.

—Letter to Charles Morton—October 9, 1950

About Ernest Hemingway he was always in two minds but the down side of the balance tipped as the years went by. In 1942 he is confiding to Blanche Knopf (October 22) that

Hemingway with his eternal sleeping bag got to be pretty damn tiresome but at least Hemingway sees it all, not just the flies on the garbage can.

And later,

Even Hemingway has let me down. I've been re-reading a lot of his stuff. I would have said here is one guy who writes like himself, and I would have been right, but not the way I meant it. Ninety percent of it is the goddamnest self-imitation. He never really wrote but one story. All the rest of it is the same thing in different pants—or without different pants.

As early as 1932—before he had begun to establish his own credentials—he had written an affectionate parody of the eminently parody-able Hemingway style ("Dedicated with no good reason to the greatest living American novelist"), which read in part:

Hank drank the alcohol and water.

    It was warm all the way down. It was warm as hell. It was warmer than whiskey. It was warmer than that Asti Spumante they had that time in Capozzo when Hank was with the Arditi. They had been carp fishing with landing nets. It had been a good day. After the fourth bottle of Asti Spumante Hank fell in the river and came out with his hair full of carp. Old Peguzzi laughed until his boots rattled on the hard grey rock. And afterward Peguzzi got gonorrhea on the Pave. It was a hell of a war.

In *Farewell, My Lovely* Chandler gives Marlowe the opportunity to joke with and about the great man. Marlowe insists on calling a puzzled bent cop "Hemingway." "Who is this Hemingway person?" the cop finally asks.

"A guy that keeps saying the same thing over and over until you begin to believe it must be good."

    "That must take a hell of a long time," the big man said.

And even that wasn't the end of his fixation with the literary Mr. Macho. In *The Little Sister* he has the nymphomaniac Dolores Gonzales ask Marlowe, "I was good in there, no?"—a typical Hemingway line—and he allows a party girl to repeat it in *The Long Goodbye.* The theory presumably being that a good line doesn't care who has it—or how often.

He had no doubts about Hemingway's contemporary and some-time competitor F. Scott Fitzgerald:

Nothing but the best will do for him. I think he just missed being a great writer, and the reason is pretty obvious. If the poor guy was already an alcoholic in his college days, it's a marvel that he did as well as he did. He had one of the rarest qualities in all literature . . . charm.

—Letter to Dale Warren—November 13, 1950

He had great admiration for Somerset Maugham as a technician, and considered *Ashenden* "so far ahead of any other spy story ever written," although Maugham's novels, "the best of them, and good as they are, do not outclass the field." The reason—Chandler felt—was because "he can never make you catch your breath or lose your head, because he never loses his. I doubt that he ever wrote a line which seemed fresh from creation, and many lesser writers have."

He has no magic and very little gusto. His style, which has been greatly praised, seems to me to be no more than a good competent mandarin English which often only narrowly escapes dullness.

—Letter to Hamish Hamilton—January 5, 1950

*F. Scott Fitzgerald
with his wife, Zelda
(1896–1940).*
Photofest

*W. Somerset Maugham
(1874–1965).*
Photofest

Which didn't prevent him from writing to Maugham a week later
to thank him for the autographed copy of *Ashenden*:

> . . . the only time I asked for or even desired such a thing from
> any author . . . I can only wish in vain that I might thank you in
> words as graceful and unique as the person to whom they would
> be addressed . . . But . . . I can only thank you quite simply and
> say that the nearness of your name to mine on the title page of a
> book is as near as I am likely to get to distinction, and a good deal
> nearer than I deserve.

> The best writing in English today is done by Americans, but not
> in any purist tradition. They have roughed the language around
> as Shakespeare did and done it the violence of melodrama . . .
> They have knocked over tombs and sneered at the dead. Which
> is as it should be. There are too many dead men and too much
> talk about them.

> —Letter to the Editor of *The Fortnightly Intruder*—July 1, 1937

One of the "dead men" who had been talked about and was—in Chandler's view—vastly overrated by the intelligentsia was playwright Eugene O'Neill, considered by many to be America's answer to Shakespeare. Chandler didn't think so . . .

> O'Neill is the sort of man who could spend a year in a flophouse, researching flophouses, and write a play about flophouses that would be no more real than a play by a man who had never been in a flophouse, but had only read about them.
> —Letter to James Sandoe—January 27, 1948

It is likely that one particular incident confirmed his feelings:

> Throughout the play *The Iceman Cometh* O'Neill uses the expression "the big sleep" as a synonym for death. He is apparently under the impression that this is a current underworld or halfworld usage, whereas it is a pure invention on my part. If I am

Eugene O'Neill (1888–1953).
Photofest

remembered long enough, I shall probably be accused of stealing
the phrase from O'Neill, since he is a big shot.
                    —Letter to Cleve Adams—September 4, 1948

But whatever his reservations about his fellow contemporary writers, as a man of letters he had an appropriate respect for one of the
immortals:

Shakespeare would have done well in any generation, because he
would have refused to die in a corner; he would have taken the
false gods and made them over, he would have taken the current
formulae and forced them into something lesser men thought
them incapable of. Alive today, he would undoubtedly have written and directed motion pictures, plays, and God knows what.
Instead of saying "This medium is not good," he would have
used it and made it good. If some people had called some of his
work cheap (which some of it is), he wouldn't have cared a rap,
because he would know that without some vulgarity there is no
complete man. He would have hated refinement, as such, because
it is always a withdrawal, a shrinking, and he was much too tough
to shrink from anything.
                    —Letter to Hamish Hamilton—April 22, 1949

Even though he was now publishing fairly regularly—twenty pulp
stories between 1933 and 1939—Chandler was not fully emotionally
committed to hard-boiled fiction, as it was popularly called. He had a
hankering to alternate it with fantasy.

His notebook contains this entry:

Since all plans are foolish and those written down are never ful-
filled, let us make a plan this 16th day of March 1939, at Riverside,
California.

   For the rest of 1939, all of 1940, spring of 1941, and then if
there is no war and if there is any money, to go to England for
material.

He then lists several projects in synopsis form and concludes,

The three mystery stories should be finished in the next two years, by the end of 1940. If they make enough for me to move to England and to forget mystery writing and try *English Summer (A Gothic Romance)* and the Fantastic Stories, without worrying about whether they make money, I'll tackle them. But I must have two years money ahead, and a sure market with the detective story when I come back to it, if I do. If *English Summer* is a smash hit, which it should be, properly written, written up to the hilt but not overwritten, I'm set for life. From then on I'll alternate the fantastic and the dramatic until I think of a new type. Or may do a suave detective just for the fun.

Cissy typed up these notes and added a P.S. of her own . . .

Dear Raymio, you'll have fun looking at this maybe, and seeing what useless dreams you had. Or perhaps it will not be fun.

As it happened, events were already shaping otherwise. In 1938 Sydney Sanders, a New York literary agent, had read and been impressed by some of Chandler's pulp stories. He persuaded publisher Alfred Knopf to commission a full-length novel.

Despite Chandler's contention that he was always a slow worker—

I work too slowly, throw away too much . . . and what I write that sells is not at all the sort of thing I really want to write.
—Letter to George Harmon Coxe—October 17, 1939

—he finished *The Big Sleep* in three months.

But a lot of the material in it was revamped from a couple of novelettes ("Killer in the Rain" and "The Curtain"). This gave it body but it didn't make it any easier to write . . . for me it was a terrific production and I have never approached it since.
—Letter to Hamish Hamilton—November 10, 1950

*Alfred and Blanche Knopf. Together they formed the Knopf publishing house in
1915.* The Harry Ransom Center, University of Texas at Austin

Knopf published the book in the United States in February 1939,
and Hamish Hamilton in the U.K. a month later. Chandler was now
fifty-one. Reviews were mainly favorable and it sold well—particularly
in the U.K., where Chandler's reputation was to be always in advance
of the one he enjoyed in America.

He remained skeptical of the publishing process:

> I have never had any great respect for the ability of editors, pub-
> lishers, play and picture producers to guess what the public will
> like . . . I have always tried to put myself in the shoes of the ulti-
> mate consumer, the reader, and ignore the middleman.
> —Letter to George Harmon Coxe—June 27, 1940

Later he would sound more ironic on the topic . . .

> But you know how ignorant the public is. Compared with an
> agent the public knows nothing.
> —Letter to Hamish Hamilton—May 25, 1952

Chandler himself was more than a little perturbed by the fact that the prestigious *New York Times* found aspects of the book unpleasant. He reflects to Knopf (February 19, 1939) that

> my fiction was learned in a rough school, and I probably didn't notice them much. I was more intrigued by a situation where the mystery is solved by the exposition and understanding of a single character, always well in evidence, rather than by the slow and sometimes long-winded concatenation of circumstances.

As for the next book that Knopf is encouraging him to produce without delay,

> I should like, if you approve, to try to jack it up a few more notches. It must be kept sharp, swift and racy, of course, but I think it could be a little less harsh . . . *The Big Sleep* is very unequally written. There are scenes that are all right, but there are other scenes

Chandler's first novel. Published by Alfred A. Knopf in the United States in February 1939.

still much too pulpy. Insofar as I am able, I want to develop an objective method—but slowly—to the point where I can carry an audience over into a genuine dramatic, even melodramatic, novel, written in a very vivid and pungent style, but not slangy or overly vernacular. I realize that this must be done cautiously and little by little, but I think it can be done. To acquire delicacy without losing power, that's the problem.

In an earlier letter to Blanche Knopf—March 15, 1942—he had tried to analyze the literary dichotomy he was never to solve to his own satisfaction:

The thing that rather gets me down is that when I write something that is tough and fast and full of mayhem and murder, I get panned for being tough and fast and full of mayhem, and then when I try to tone down a bit and develop the mental and emotional side of the situation, I get panned for leaving out what I was panned for putting in the first time. The reader expects thus and thus of Chandler because he did it before, but when he did it before he was informed that it might have been much better if he hadn't.

Despite his own doubts, the growing band of Chandleristas would grant him both delicacy and power as he became what *Time* magazine called "the Poet Laureate of the loner."

Without even realizing it, he had already created something that would ensure his literary legacy . . .

A man called Marlowe.

Three

Philip Marlowe
Investigations

Down these mean streets a man must go who is not himself mean, who is neither tarnished nor afraid . . . He is the hero, he is everything. He must be a complete man, and a common man and yet an unusual man. He must be . . . a man of honor, by instinct, by inevitability, without thought of it, and certainly without saying it. He must be the best man in the world, and good enough for any world . . .

—"The Simple Art of Murder"

Marlowe wouldn't be Marlowe, if he could really get along with policemen.

—Letter to Roger Machell—October 14, 1958

"The first time we met I told you I was a detective. Get it through your lovely head. I work at it, lady. I don't play at it."

—Marlowe to Vivian Regan in *The Big Sleep*

"Phil Marlowe . . . the shop-soiled Galahad."

—Dr. Carl Moss in *The High Window*

"A dirty little man in a dirty little world."

—Jules Amthor in *Farewell, My Lovely*

"You know something, Marlowe? I could get to like you. You're a bit of a bastard—like me."

—Roger Wade in *The Long Goodbye*

"Tell her to jump in the lake . . . Tell her to jump in two lakes, if one won't hold her. Not clever, but quick."

—*The High Window*

Marlowe on Marlowe:

"Marlowe knows everything—except how to make a decent living."

—*The High Window*

I was a blank man. I had no face, no meaning, no personality, hardly a name . . . I was a page from yesterday's calendar crumpled at the bottom of the waste basket.

—*The Little Sister*

Lauren Bacall and Humphrey Bogart in The Big Sleep *(1946).* Photofest

If I had ever had an opportunity of selecting the movie actor who would best represent [Marlowe] to my mind, I think it would have been Cary Grant.

—Letter to D. J. Ibberson—April 19, 1951

Marlowe is a more honorable man than you and I. I don't mean Bogart playing Marlowe and I don't mean because I created him. I didn't create him at all. I've seen dozens like him in all essentials except the few colorful qualities needed to be in a book. (A few even had those.) They were all poor. How could they be anything else?

—Letter to John Houseman—October 1949

The Private Eye inhabits that limbo land between the private citizen and the public law. Chandler and the rest of the school of "hard-boiled" writers found it necessary and profitable to glamorize the stereotype, but Chandler, at least, always recognized the truth:

Your private detective in real life is usually either an ex-policeman with a lot of hard practical experience or else a shabby little hack who runs around trying to find out where people have moved to.

The cops themselves are in no doubt about his place on the food chain. Lieutenant Reavis in "Mandarin's Jade" (1937) lays it out for P.I. John Dalmas:

"I'd like to sell you an idea, shamus. Maybe I can. There's a lot of peace of mind in it. The Police Board gave you a license once and the sheriff gave you a special badge. Any acting captain with a peeve can get both of them taken away from you overnight. Maybe even just lieutenant—like me. Now what did you have when you got that license and that badge? You had the social standing of a cockroach. You were a snooper for hire. All in the world you had to do was to spend your last hundred bucks on a down payment on some rent and office furniture and sit on your tail until somebody brought a lion in—so you could put your head in the lion's mouth to see if he would bite. If he bit your ear off, you got sued for mayhem. Are you beginning to get it? "

Greystone Mansion, Beverly Hills—inspiration for the Sternwood Mansion in The Big Sleep.

To which Dalmas predictably replies:

"It's a good line," I said. "I used it years ago. So you don't want to break the case?"

Then John Dalmas begat Philip Marlowe. Marlowe was "no one person." He "just grew out of the pulps."

Nonetheless, he became very much "one person." He was to have been called Mallory—not Marlowe—and for Chandler's first two *Black Mask* stories in 1933 ("Blackmailers Don't Shoot" and "Smart-Aleck Kill") he did carry that name, along with his .38 Colt. It's tempting to think the influence on this classically educated author was Sir Thomas Malory of medieval *Morte d'Arthur* fame, especially when the chivalry connection is carried through to Marlowe's beloved game of chess.

In reality he was probably, and more prosaically, named after Marlowe House at Dulwich—though several critics have tried to draw a parallel with Conrad's Marlowe in *The Heart of Darkness* (1902).

In *The Big Sleep* Chandler's White Knight—and alter ego— contemplates a game he is about to lose through making the wrong move: "Knights had no meaning in this game. It wasn't a game for knights."

He says that because it's the thing Philip Marlowe expects to hear himself say, but it's not principle that drives him. More typical is his reaction earlier in the same novel when he visits the invalid General Sternwood for the first time:

> Over the entrance doors . . . there was a broad stained-glass panel showing a knight in dark armor rescuing a lady who was tied to a tree . . . I stood there and thought that if I lived in the house I would sooner or later have to climb up there and help him out. He didn't seem to be really trying.

Marlowe never stopped trying. He may not always have slain all the dragons and rescued all the maidens, but he was never defeated.

Ironically, when he leaves the Sternwood house, having solved the case, "the knight in the stained-glass window still wasn't getting anywhere untying the naked damsel from the tree."

The Big Sleep. *Hamish Hamilton, London, 1939.*

The Lady in the Lake. *Hamish Hamilton, 1944.*

Chandler in 1939—the year
The Big Sleep *awoke real interest*
in him as more than just another
writer of "hard-boiled fiction."
Photofest

Chandler never claimed to have invented the private eye. Pulp fiction had spewed them out by the dozen—hard-boiled, laconic, treat-'em-rough-and-tell-'em-nothing. He was happy to admit that Dashiell Hammett had defined the genre and put a memorable face to it—first with his "Continental Op" and, more memorably, in *The Maltese Falcon* (1930) with Sam Spade, a character created several years before Chandler began to write crime fiction and nine years before Marlowe's debut in a full-length novel.

In retrospect one can see that from the outset Marlowe had a dimension that Spade and the others lacked. He was a realist instead of a cynic, and he was cursed with a brand of idealism that would draw him irresistibly down the meanest of mean streets.

He emerged from a whole series of Chandler predecessors in the short stories. Apart from Mallory, there was Carmady ("The Man Who Liked Dogs," "Killer in the Rain" and "The Curtain"); John Dalmas ("Mandarin's Jade" and "Bay City Blues") and John Evans ("No Crime in the Mountains"). The last of these was published in 1941, *after* Marlowe's debut, and perhaps indicates that the lack of critical response to *The Big Sleep* (1939) and *Farewell, My Lovely* (1940) had blinded him to the fact that he had already created one of crime fiction's immortals. (It was only later that the heroes of several of the earlier stories were retrospectively rechristened Marlowe.)

The difference today is apparent. Even Joseph Shaw, the editor Chandler and Hammett had in common—the editor of *Black Mask* magazine—could observe that Hammett never really cared for any of his characters, whereas it became increasingly clear that Marlowe was a Chandler alter ego. The "anti-romantic romance hero," as one critic put it; "the American mind," as Chandler himself once said.

Critics have argued—as critics will inevitably argue in an attempt to create a sociological context—that the rise of the private eye was an attempt to personalize the individual's rejection of the social and political corruption of the 1920s and '30s, but that is to miss the real point of Marlowe and to misunderstand the author. Chandler had no—what we might now call—"political agenda." He was a man out of time and place, to all intents and purposes an uprooted Edwardian Englishman attempting to make sense of an alien land and culture, "a man who loved England well when his heart was young and has never loved in the same way since, nor ever shall."

His hero, Marlowe, is—among many other things—a knight errant on a crusade in a strange land, charged to uphold the eternal values or lay down his life and honor in the attempt.

Piecing his biography together from the various clues Chandler leaves lying around, we find that Philip Marlowe would appear to have been born around 1905, although by *The Long Goodbye* (1953) he admits to being forty-two and "spoiled by independence." He was an only child, brought up in the Northern California town of Santa Rosa by parents both of whom had died by the time he became a private investigator in 1925.

At high school he played football, broke his nose ("a slight miscalculation in an attempt to block a punt") and had an operation for a deviated septum. An autobiographical touch here. In describing himself to a correspondent years later, Chandler wrote, "My nose is not sharp but blunt, the result of trying to tackle a man as he was kicking a ball."

Marlowe had "a couple of years" of college ("I can still speak English if there's any demand for it. There isn't much in my trade"—*The Big Sleep*), before attending the University of Oregon.

In this, as in so much else, he understates the facts. He must certainly have packed a fair amount of reading into those two years, since we never find him reading during his cases. At various times he quotes *Alice,* Proust, Hemingway, *Wuthering Heights,* Anatole France, T. S. Eliot, Jane Austen, Flaubert, Pepys's diaries; he paraphrases *Othello* (when he says that Mr. Grayle in *Farewell, My Lovely* was "an old man who had loved wisely, but not too well") and—in the same book—can wax decidedly lyrical under the influence of drugs:

> "Speak out, Dr. Fell. Pluck the antique viol, let the soft music float . . . But me no buts. I'll make a sop of you, I'll drown you in a butt of Malmsey wine."

On occasion the lyrical phrases are all his own:

> "You have been drinking," she said slowly.
> "Only Chanel No. 5, and kisses, and the pale glow of lovely legs, and the mocking invitation in deep blue eyes. Innocent things like that."
> —*The Little Sister*

> "Never the time and the place and the loved one all together," I said . . . "Browning. The poet, not the automatic."
> —*The Little Sister*

Though when he was playing scrupulously by his sardonic rules, it didn't do to admit to too much literacy. When Marlowe arrives at his office in *The Big Sleep,* he finds Vivian Regan waiting for him.

> "I was beginning to think perhaps you worked in bed, like Marcel Proust."
> "Who's he?" I put a cigarette in my mouth and stared at her.

Art, on the other hand—particularly modern art—smacks of pretension all too often for Marlowe's taste . . .

"I picked it up just the other day, Asta Dial's *Spirit of Dawn.*"
"I thought it was Klopstein's *Two Warts on a Fanny,*" I said . . .
"You have a somewhat peculiar sense of humor," he said.
"Not peculiar," I said. "Just uninhibited."

—*Farewell, My Lovely*

A couple of vigorously colored daubs on the walls that looked lousy enough to have cost money.

—*The Little Sister*

. . . and music didn't fare much better:

I was . . . listening to Khachaturyan working in a tractor factory. He called it a violin concerto. I called it a loose fan belt and the hell with it.

—*The Long Goodbye*

Kropp's Piano Concerto for Two Lame Thumbs.

On the other hand, he *does* like Mozart!

He worked as a field investigator for an insurance company before joining the office of the Los Angeles D.A., Taggart Wilde. ("I was fired for insubordination. I test very high on insubordination"—*The Big Sleep*.) Chandler speculated that Marlowe was "too efficient at a time and in a place where efficiency was the last thing desired by the persons in charge." He was never a regular cop, although he knew the breed well and a career-long friend was Bernie Ohls, one of the D.A.'s key investigators.

He runs afoul of the law on numerous occasions and occasionally pays the inevitable price for protecting his client. ("I've been in jail more than once.")

Why did Marlowe come to Los Angeles? Chandler said he was

never sure himself, except that "eventually most people do, although not all of them remain."

He stands six feet and a half-inch tall and at the time of *The Big Sleep* (1939) weighs 190 pounds. He may have added three or four pounds over the years. His hair is dark brown, although by *The Lady in the Lake* (1943) "I brushed my hair and looked at the gray in it. There was getting to be plenty of gray in it." He has "warm brown eyes with flecks of gold in them"—but then that is a lady noticing them.

"Well, you got a build on you for the work," he said, satisfied. "And your face don't tell a lot of stories."

—*The Lady in the Lake*

In the early short stories he pays little attention to his appearance and habitually wears a "shiny blue serge suit" ("Goldfish"—1936), but for his debut in a full-length novel, *The Big Sleep,* three years later, he takes more pains:

Audrey Totter and Robert Montgomery star in La Dame du Lac/The Lady in the Lake *(1946).* Belgian poster

It was about eleven o'clock in the morning, mid-October, with the sun not shining and a look of hard wet rain in the clearness of the foothills. I was wearing my powder-blue suit with dark shirt, tie and display handkerchief, black brogues, black wool socks with dark blue clocks on them. I was neat, clean, shaved and sober, and I didn't care who knew it.

In the mid-1930s he has an office in the Condor Building but soon moves to the mythical Cahuenga Building—first to the seventh floor, then settling on the sixth (Suite 615): "two small rooms at the back," the smaller of them "the half-office I use for a Reception Room" with "a buzzer on the door which I could switch on and off from my private thinking parlor" ("my down-at-the-heels brain emporium").

The pebbled glass door panel is lettered in flaked black paint: "Philip Marlowe . . . Investigations." It is a reasonably shabby door at the end of a reasonably shabby corridor in the sort of building that was new about the year the all-tile bathroom became the basis of civilization.

As I walked into the musty silence of the little waiting-room there was the usual feeling of having been dropped down a well dried up twenty years ago to which no one would come back ever. The smell of old dust hung in the air as flat and stale as a football interview.

I opened the inner door and inside there it was the same dead air, the same dust along the veneer, the same broken promise of a life of ease.

In *The Big Sleep* the reception area has a "faded red settee, two odd semi-easy chairs, the net curtains that needed laundering ["I'll send them only come St. Swithin's Day"—*Farewell, My Lovely*] and the boy's size library table with the venerable magazines on it to give the place a professional touch." By *The High Window* the magazines are "dead" and the room, with its "rusty floor covering and the general air of not much money being made," is "empty of everything but dust."

The door was invariably left unlocked "for a client to go in and wait, in case I had a client, and the client cared to sit down and wait."

In the office itself, with its "mustard yellow plaster wall," were:

> A rust-red carpet, not very young, five green filing cases, three of them full of California climate, an advertising calendar showing the Quints rolling around on a sky-blue floor, in pink dresses, with seal-brown hair and sharp black eyes as large as mammoth prunes. There were three near-walnut chairs, the usual desk with the usual blotter, pen set, ashtray and telephone, and the usual squeaky swivel chair behind it.
>
> —*The Big Sleep*—1939

> Three hard chairs and a swivel chair, a flat desk with a glass top, five green filing cabinets, three of them full of nothing, a calendar, and a framed license bond on the wall, a washbowl in a stained wooden cupboard, a hatrack, a carpet that was just something on

Detection starts at home. Robert Montgomery as Marlowe clearly hasn't noticed that whoever inscribed his office window called him "Phillip" instead of "Philip"—and that his favorite newspaper prefers "clews" to "clues." Photofest

The Dionne Quintuplets, born in Ontario, Canada, in May 1934. Photofest

the floor, and two open windows with net curtains that puckered in and out like the lips of a toothless old man sleeping. The same stuff I had last year, and the year before that. Not beautiful, not gay, but better than a tent on the beach.

—*The High Window*—1942

By the time of *The Little Sister* (1948) the five green filing cases have been reduced to three and we are introduced to:

the light fixture in the ceiling with three dead moths in it that had been there for at least six months . . . grimy woodwork and the pen set on the desk and tired, tired telephone (on which he liked to hang his hat instead of bothering with the hat-rack) . . . the Boston sharpener screwed to the edge of the window frame.

Little changes over the years.

The desk acquires a "stained brown blotter" and a desk lighter, together with a holder for a range of pipes including a bulldog. One drawer of the desk holds a fresh pack of cigarettes (usually Camels at fifteen cents a pack!—although "almost any cigarette will satisfy

. . . although "almost any cigarette will satisfy him." (And in The Long Goodbye *he's even caught smoking a "bulldog pipe.")*

him") and a duster; and in the deep bottom drawer is a bottle of whiskey (usually Old Forester) and "two pony glasses"—in case he should happen to have a visitor and the visitor should also happen to be thirsty.

In *The High Window* it's Old Taylor. At home he's been known to keep Four Roses.

Marlowe's drinking habits, incidentally—rather like his own—were a subject that could make Chandler testy. While Marlowe rarely turned down a bourbon or rye when it was offered—and had been known to help himself on occasion when it was not—it wasn't his only tipple ("I was never fussy about drinks"). His preferred cocktail seems to have been a double Gibson, or the gimlets he drinks with Terry Lennox in *The Long Goodbye*. Chandler once claimed to a correspondent that the P.I. "didn't prefer rye to bourbon and would drink practically anything that is not sweet . . . Certain drinks such as Pink Ladies, Honolulu cocktails and *crème de menthe* highballs he would regard as an insult." However, "I am a little tired of the numerous suggestions that . . . he's always full of whiskey . . . When he wants a drink he takes it openly and doesn't hesitate to remark on it. I don't know how it is in your part of the country, but compared with the country-club set in my part of the country he is as sober as a deacon" (Letter to a fan—October 1951).

Although in 1945 Chandler had referred to him as "a simple alcoholic vulgarian who never sleeps with his clients while on duty."

"Alcohol is like love," [Terry] said. "The first kiss is magic, the second is intimate, the third is routine. After that you take the girl's clothes off."

"Is that bad?" I asked him.

—*The Long Goodbye*

"I think a man ought to get drunk at least twice a year just on principle, so he won't let himself get snotty about it."

—Raymond Chandler

"His guns have been rather various. He started out with a German Luger automatic pistol. He seems to have had Colt automatics of various calibers, but not larger than .38 and when last I heard he has a Smith & Wesson .38 Special, probably with a four inch barrel. This is a very powerful gun . . . and has the advantage over an automatic of using a lead cartridge. It will not jam or discharge accidentally . . . and is probably just as effective a weapon at short range as a .45 caliber automatic" (Raymond Chandler).

The top left-hand drawer was reserved for his gun—initially a Luger, then later a Colt .38 or a Smith & Wesson .38 with a 4-inch barrel. To make life easier he would also have a .38 in the glove compartment of whatever car he was driving and a pint of Old Forester to keep it company. On the job he invariably "carried" in a shoulder holster.

The rest of his professional equipment consisted of a photostat of his P.I. license, an honorary deputy sheriff's badge with a set of phony business cards (ditto), a penknife and a fountain-pen flashlight.

"I'm not too fussy about cars," he would claim and he tended to hang onto them. Back in 1934 (*Finger Man*) the car was "still" a 1925 Mar-

Marlowe's "assistants": "I knew one thing: as soon as anyone said you didn't need a gun, you'd better take one along that worked." Colt .38 Super Match (top).

"The muzzle of the Luger looked like the mouth of the Second Street tunnel" (The Big Sleep). Luger P08 (Parabellum) (middle), Smith & Wesson .38 (with 4" barrel) (bottom).

"I'm not too fussy about cars." —Marlowe

Top to bottom: Marmon 34 Touring Car, Oldsmobile Series 60, 1937 Chrysler Airflow.

mon Touring Car. Ten years later, in *The Lady in the Lake,* he's traded it in for a Chrysler, and by 1953 (*The Long Goodbye*) he's driving an Oldsmobile. He's also become socially mobile—the latest office block gives him a parking space!

> "I read somewhere that a dick should always have a plain, dark, inconspicuous car that nobody would notice. The guy had never been to L.A. In L.A. to be conspicuous you would have to drive a flesh-pink Mercedes-Benz with a sun-porch on the roof and three pretty girls sun-bathing."
>
> —*Playback*

The office—which opens onto an "imitation marble corridor"—would eventually acquire "a small radio in the corner beyond the edge of the desk" and a leather cigar humidor for his Pearce's mixture "from an admirer" ("by an odd coincidence having the same name as me," he admits), while the stained wooden cupboard with the open door now boasts "a flawed mirror."

By *The Long Goodbye* it also has a fan ("It didn't make the air any cooler, just a little more lively") and a Boston fern that needs watering. ("I think it needs re-potting too," Linda Loring tells him. "Too many air roots.") At no time does it boast the luxury of a secretary or an answering service.

Naturally, a change of year dictated a change of calendar. Out go the Dionne Quintuplets, and in *Farewell, My Lovely* (1940):

> Rembrandt was on the calendar that year, a rather smeary self-portrait due to imperfectly registered color plates. It showed him holding a smeared palette with a dirty thumb and wearing a tam-o'-shanter which wasn't any too clean either. His other hand held a brush poised in the air, as if he might be going to do a little work after a while, if somebody made a down payment. His face was aging, saggy, full of the disgust of life and the thickening effects of liquor. But it had a hard cheerfulness that I liked, as the eyes were as bright as drops of dew.

Marlowe's apartment building on Hightower Drive.

As for that visitor's chair—"A lot of people had tried to get comfortable in that chair. I ought to try it myself some time. Maybe it was losing business for me."

Marlowe had plenty of time on his hands to study the current calendar, the mustard yellow plaster wall and the rust-red carpet, but occasionally his contemplation was enlivened by a little nature study:

> I had been stalking the bluebottle fly for five minutes, waiting for him to sit down. He didn't want to sit down. He just wanted to do wing-overs and sing the prologue to *Pagliacci*.
>
> —*The Little Sister*

Leaving the windows open made the neighbors a definite factor. Across the alley on the opposite side of the air shaft was the Mansion House Hotel, a paradigm of the air pollution that was changing the City of Angels beyond recognition. Soot from its oil burners was "rolling across the glass top of the desk in tiny particles, like pollen drifting over a vacant lot" ("Goldfish"). In *The Big Sleep*—three years later—the analogy had changed: "Soot . . . was down-drafted into the room and rolling across the top of the desk like tumbleweed drifting across a vacant lot."

But it wasn't just the dust . . .

The fish smell from the Mansion House coffee shop was strong enough to build a garage on.

—*Farewell, My Lovely*

Despite that, he eats there regularly. Haute cuisine is not among Marlowe's affectations. "I gobbled what they called the regular dinner, drank a brandy to sit on its chest" (*The Lady in the Lake*).

"Bad but quick. Feed 'em and throw 'em out. Lots of business. We can't bother with you sitting over your second cup of coffee, mister, you're using money space."

—*The Long Goodbye*

I went down to the drugstore and ate a chicken salad sandwich and drank some coffee. The coffee was over-strained and the sandwich was as full of rich flavor as a piece of old shirt. Americans will eat anything if it is toasted and held together with a couple of toothpicks and has lettuce sticking out of the sides, preferably a little wilted.

—*The Long Goodbye*

The eighty-five cent dinner tasted like a discarded mail-bag and was served to me by a waiter who looked as if he would slug me for a quarter, cut my throat for six bits and bury me at sea in a barrel of concrete for a dollar and a half plus sales tax.

—*Farewell, My Lovely*

Down at the drug-store lunch counter I had time to inhale two cups of coffee and a melted cheese sandwich with two slivers of

ersatz bacon embedded in it, like dead fish in the silt at the bottom of a drained pool.

—*The Little Sister*

By 1959 ("The Pencil") he is patronizing Joe's Eats next door. The
cuisine maintains the Marlowe standards:

> "All I want is two eggs three minutes—no more—a slice of your
> famous concrete toast, a tall glass of tomato juice with a dash of
> Lea and Perrins, a big happy smile and don't give anybody else my
> coffee. I might need it all."
>
> . . . I got the eggs the way I liked them. The toast had been
> painted with melted butter past its bloom.
>
> "No Lea and Perrins," she said, putting down the tomato juice.
> "How about a little Tabasco? We're fresh out of arsenic, too."
>
> I used two drops of Tabasco, swallowed the eggs, drank two
> cups of coffee and was about to leave the toast for a tip, but I went
> soft and left a quarter instead.

In whatever apartment he was currently calling home, Marlowe
prided himself on keeping a neat kitchen, even though he used it
mainly to make breakfast and frequent strong coffee, something on
which he rather prided himself. He refers to the drinking of it as taking a conference with "Mr. Huggins and Mr. Young"—a play on the
name of a brand popular at the time.

"You don't put on much of a front," Vivian Regan tells him in *The
Big Sleep*, verbalizing what many of his clients must have thought over
the years.

Linda Loring echoes it in *The Long Goodbye*:

> "Your establishment isn't exactly palatial," she said. "Don't you
> even have a secretary?"
>
> "It's a sordid life, but I'm used to it."

Nor is Marlowe's apartment anything to write home about. In
"Finger Man"(1934) he is staying at the Merritt Plaza in a single apart-

ment with a pull-down Murphy bed; four years later in "Red Wind" at the Berglund; but *The Big Sleep* (1939) finds him at the Hobart Arms on Franklin near Kenmore, paying something like sixty dollars a month, furnished.

This was the room I had to live in. It was all I had in the way of a home. In it was everything that took the place of a family. Not much; a few books, pictures, radio, chessmen, old letters, stuff like that. Nothing. Such as they were they had all my memories.

Chess is a Marlowe hobby over the years. He has "a small polished table with its inlaid squares of brown and pale gold," on which he sets

Marlowe's taste in coffee. He gives a glowing commercial for it as he makes a cup for a "gentleman" who is pointing a gun at him in The Long Goodbye. *"Mr. Huggins and Mr. Young are two of the best. They make Huggins-Young coffee for me. It's their life work, their pride and joy. One of these days I'm going to see that they get the recognition they deserve. So far all they're making is money."*

In the bottom drawer of Marlowe's desk lurks a bottle of whiskey—usually Old Forester—and "two pony glasses," in case he had a visitor and the visitor should happen to be thirsty. At home it might be Old Grand-Dad or Four Roses.

out the classic games he plays against himself. At the end of *The High Window* he finds refuge in "beautiful cold, remorseless chess, almost creepy in its silent implacability" and toasts the great game—" 'You and Capablanca,' I said."

On another occasion, though, he views the game with more typical irony and himself for taking it so seriously. It is, he says,

> a prize specimen of the irresistible force meeting the immovable object, a battle without armor, a war without blood, and as elaborate a waste of human intelligence as you could find anywhere outside an advertising agency.
>
> —*The Long Goodbye*

In *The High Window* (1942) he has moved to Apartment 408 in the Bristol Apartment Building, 1634 North Bristol Avenue, Hollywood (Glenview 7537), but there is no indication that he has upgraded.

By *The Long Goodbye* (1953) he has a year's rental—"in a house in Yucca Avenue. It was a small hillside house on a dead-end street with a long flight of redwood steps to the front door and a grove of eucalyptus trees across the way." He rented it furnished but the cat-pee smell of the eucalyptus in bloom clearly didn't appeal, and by *Playback* (1958) he is back in one-room mode:

> I'm a tired hack with a doubtful future . . . Wherever I went, whatever I did, this was what I'd come back to. A blank wall in a meaningless room in a meaningless house.
>
> —*Playback*

"I'm a lone wolf," he tells publisher Howard Spencer in *The Long Goodbye,* "unmarried, getting middle-aged and not rich. I like liquor and women and chess and a few other things."

> "The client is always mister to me . . . Until he has told me a few dozen lies anyway."
>
> —*The Long Goodbye*

"I'm selling what I have to make a living. What little guts and intelligence the Lord gave me and a willingness to get pushed around in order to protect a client."

—*The Big Sleep*

Professionally Marlowe sets his own idiosyncratic rules. He refuses divorce work but will take anything else that is legal. As far as money is concerned, "There's not much money in it. There's a lot of grief. But there's a lot of fun, too." (*Farewell, My Lovely*) . . . "You can't make much money at this trade, if you're honest." (*The Big Sleep*) . . . "I'm not an organization. I'm just one man and I work at just one case at a time. I take risks, sometimes quite big risks, and I don't work all the time." (*The High Window*)

His going rate is twenty-five dollars a day and expenses; he charges eight cents a mile for his car. " 'Trouble is my business,' I said. 'Twenty-five a day and a guarantee of two-fifty, if I pull the job.' " ("Trouble Is My Business"—1939). By *The Little Sister* (1948) it's "forty bucks a day and expenses. Unless it's a job that can be done for a flat fee . . . That's the asking price. I take twenty-five. I've taken less." In *Playback* (1958): "For fifty bucks a day I don't get shot. That costs seventy-five."

Because he reckons his fee is fair, Marlowe takes exception to people who can well afford it but try to beat down the price:

"All I have the itch for is money. I am so money greedy that for twenty-five bucks a day and expenses, mostly gasoline and whiskey, I do my thinking myself, what there is of it. I risk my whole future, what there is of it, the hatred of the cops . . . I dodge bullets and eat saps, and say thank you very much, if you have any more trouble, I hope you'll think of me, I'll just leave one of my cards, in case anything comes up. I do all this for twenty-five bucks a day."

—*The Big Sleep*

And should a client persist in arguing—as the prissy Miss Orfamay Quest does in *The Little Sister*:

"Have you ever looked at the dust jacket for The Little Sister? *It portrays a dessicated school teacher or librarian of some 38 or 40 years of age, about as sexy as a rat-trap. Yet this little girl was young and without her glasses or with smarter ones looked good enough to fumble with. Some day, just for the hell of it, a dust jacket artist ought to submit to the excruciating agony of reading the damn book."* —Letter to Hamish Hamilton—October 26, 1956

"Don't bother about the twenty bucks. You can have it back, if you like. I didn't even bruise it."

Then she straightened the bills out on the desk . . . very slowly, very sadly, as if she was drowning a favorite kitten.

I'm in the hide-and-seek business . . . I was doing a cheap sneaky job for people I didn't like but—that's what you hire out for, chum. They pay the bills, you dig the dirt.

—*Playback*

"What's the most you ever made on a single job?"

"Eight-fifty."

"Jesus, how cheap can a guy get?"

—*The Long Goodbye*

But whatever he did, he had no illusions that he would ever be a rich man:

"My bank account was still trying to crawl under a duck . . ."
—*Farewell, My Lovely*

As late as *The Long Goodbye* he had only "twelve hundred dollars in the bank and a few thousands in bonds," while in "The Pencil," "My checking account could kiss the sidewalk without stooping."

"I'm a romantic," he tells Bernie Ohls in *The Long Goodbye*. "I hear crying in the night and I go see what's the matter . . . but no money, not a dime . . . But I can always tell a cop to go to hell. Go to hell, Bernie . . ."

"You boys are as cute as a couple of lost golf-balls," I said.
—*The High Window*

But in Marlowe's book, when you took the money, you did the job . . .

"You're my client—five thousand dollars' worth. I have to do something for it—even if it's no more than growing a mustache."
—*Playback*

"I'd like to be smooth and distant and subtle . . . I'd like to play the sort of game just once the way somebody like you would like it to be played. But nobody will let me—not the clients, nor the cops, nor the people I played against. However hard I try to be nice I always end up with my nose in the dirt and my thumb feeling for somebody's eye."
—*The Lady in the Lake*

"I don't think he's a real dick. He don't seem to throw his weight enough."
—Of P.I. John Evans in "No Crime in the Mountains"

"You a real dick or just a shamus?" Marlowe is asked in *The Lady in the Lake*. "Just a shamus." But a shamus who defines his own code, marches to his own drummer and takes what he does seriously.

"Private investigator, huh?" he said thoughtfully. "What kind of work do you do mostly?"

"Anything that's reasonably honest," I said.

He nodded. "Reasonably is a word you could stretch. So is honest."

—*The Little Sister*

"You in show business?"

"Just the opposite of show business. I'm in the hide-and-seek business."

—*Playback*

"I heard you leveled with the customers, Marlowe."

"That's why I stay poor."

—"The Pencil"

I needed a drink, I needed a lot of life insurance, I needed a vacation, I needed a home in the country. What I had was a coat, a hat and a gun. I put them on and went out of the room.

—*Farewell, My Lovely*

"Well, what is my business? Do I know? Did I ever know?"

—*The Little Sister*

I'm a fellow who likes to take an idea over by the light and have a good look at it.

—*The Little Sister*

"I'm in a business where people come to me with troubles. Big troubles, little troubles, but always troubles they don't want to take to the cops . . ."

What makes a man stay with it nobody knows. You don't get rich, you don't often have much fun. Sometimes you get beaten up or shot at or tossed into the jailhouse. Once in a long while you get dead . . . Then the door buzzer rings and you open the inner door to the waiting room and there stands a new face with a new problem, a new load of grief, and a small piece of money.

—The Long Goodbye

"If I get knocked off, put just one red rose on my grave. I don't like cut flowers. I like to see them grow."

—"The Pencil"

Why the hell hadn't I got myself a government job ten years ago? Make it fifteen. I had brains enough to get a mail-order law degree.

—"The Pencil"

"Dick," "shamus," "keyhole peeper," "eye," "gumshoe," they were all names that meant nothing to Marlowe. Apart from drawing the line at divorce work, his approach to his work was eminently pragmatic. ("Once in a while in my business a man has to do a good deal of taking"—*Playback*) (" 'Some days I feel like playing it smooth,' I said, 'and some days I feel like playing it like a waffle iron.' "—"Trouble Is My Business"):

"When you hire a boy in my line of work it isn't like hiring a window-washer and showing him eight windows and saying: 'Wash those and you're through.' *You* don't know what I have to go through or over or under to do your job for you. I do it my way. I do my best to protect you and I may break a few rules, but I do break them in your favor. The client comes first, unless he's crooked. Even then all I do is hand the job back and keep my mouth shut.

". . . I'm not Sherlock Holmes or Philo Vance. I don't expect to go over ground the police have covered and pick up a broken pen point and build a case from it. If you think there is anybody in the detective business making a living doing that sort of thing, you don't know much about cops."

—The Big Sleep

"All right," he said wearily. "Get on with it. I have a feeling you are going to be very brilliant. Remorseless flow of logic and intuition and all that rot. Just like a detective in a book."

"Sure. Taking the evidence piece by piece, putting it all together in a neat pattern, sneaking in an odd bit I had on my hip here and there, analyzing the motives and characters and making them out to be quite different from what anybody—or I myself for that matter—thought them to be up to this golden moment—and finally making a sort of world-weary pounce on the least promising suspect."

He lifted his eyes and almost smiled. "Who thereupon turns as pale as paper, froths at the mouth, and pulls a gun out of his right ear."

—The High Window

Bad cops hate him but the better ones have his measure. In *The High Window* one of them quotes his boss's verdict:

"[He] says you are not as smart as you think you are, but that you are a guy things happen to, and a guy like that could be a lot more trouble than a very smart guy."

Marlowe relied on his instincts and they rarely let him down . . .

It is like a sudden scream in the night, but there is no sound. Almost always at night, because the dark hours are the hours of danger. But it happened to me also in broad daylight—that strange, clarified moment when I suddenly know something I have no reason for knowing . . . the abrupt certainty that what bullfighters call "the moment of truth" is here.

—Playback

The Marlowe manner was invariably direct, especially when the other person was playing games. "I don't mind if you don't like my manners," he tells Vivian Regan in *The Big Sleep.* "They're pretty bad. I grieve over them during the long winter evenings."

"I figured I'd find out if you were smart enough to be worth talking to."

"I'm very smart," I said. "It would be a shame not to talk to me."

—*The High Window*

"Nothing I say is nice. I'm not nice."

—*The Little Sister*

I grinned at her sadly. "I know I talk too smart. It's in the air nowadays."

—*Farewell, My Lovely*

"I've got friends who could cut you down so small you'd need a step ladder to put your shoes on."

"Somebody did a lot of hard work on that one," I said. "But hard work's no substitute for talent."

—*Playback*

"I'm afraid I don't like your manner."

"I've had complaints about it," I said. "But nothing seems to do any good."

—*Farewell, My Lovely*

Saying the wrong thing is one of my specialties.

—"The Pencil"

"You're Marlowe?"

I nodded.

"I'm a little disappointed," he said, "I rather expected something with dirty fingernails."

"Come inside," I said, "and you can be witty sitting down."

—*The High Window*

"Does all this figuring ever get you anywhere?"

"No. It's just something to do while I'm patting the cold cream into my face at night."

—"Bay City Blues"

In a conversation with hoodlum Eddie Mars, Mars asks him:

"Is that any of your business, soldier?"
  "I could make it my business."
  "And I could make your business my business."
  "You wouldn't like it. The pay's too small."

—*The Big Sleep*

"I made no remark," he said.
  "Remarks want you to make them," I said.

—*Farewell, My Lovely*

"I can see," Breeze said, "that you know a lot about dames."
  "Not knowing a lot about them has helped me in my business."

—*The High Window*

"American girls are terrific. American wives take in too damn much territory."

—*The Long Goodbye*

The one-liner often proved more potent than the gun: "Always the wisecrack where possible" (*The Little Sister*). And besides, "Guns never settle anything. They are just a fast curtain to a bad second act."

—*Playback*

I took the wrinkles out of my lips and said aloud: "Hello, again. Anybody here needing a detective?"

—*Playback*

"He wouldn't hurt a fly, really."
  "Next time you come up I'll have one for him not to hurt. "

—*The Little Sister*

I offered him a buck but he wouldn't take it. I offered to buy him the poems of T. S. Eliot. He said he already had them.

—*The Long Goodbye*

"For ten dollars I could sing like four canaries and a steel guitar."

"I don't like these plushy orchestrations," I said.

—*The High Window*

"You talk too much," she said.

"Yes," I said. "I talk too much. Lonely men always talk too much. Either that or they don't talk at all."

—*The Little Sister*

"I don't drink until sundown. That way you don't get to be a heel."

"Tough on the Eskimos," I said. "In the summertime, anyway."

—"Goldfish"

"Oh, a lot of women keep throwing their arms around my neck and fainting on me and getting kissed and so forth. Quite a full couple of days for a beat-up gumshoe with no yacht."

—*The Little Sister*

"Why, the thing stands out so far you could break off a yard of it and still have enough left for a baseball bat."

"I ought to have said that one," I said. "Just my style."

—*Farewell, My Lovely*

Chandler clearly had as much fun putting the gags into Marlowe's mouth as if he had delivered them himself, and as the years went by they came zinging out like bullets. Even more so after he'd become a screenplay writer:

My tendency to gag is undoubtedly the influence of Hollywood, which I struggled against to the best of my ability . . . Shakespeare does it too, does it all the time. He just does it better.

—Letter to James Sandoe—September 14, 1949

So, when advising the writers of a radio series based on Marlowe, he has clear guidelines in mind for them:

Don't have Marlowe say things merely to score off the other characters. When he comes out with a smart wisecrack it should be jerked out of him emotionally, so that he is discharging an emotion and not even thinking about laying anyone out with a sharp retort ... There should not be any effect of gloating ... Too many first person characters give an offensively cocky impression. That's bad. To avoid that you must not always give him the punch line or the exit line. Not even often.

What makes Marlowe endearing—and sets him apart from the smart-aleck, hard-boiled heroes that have come to infest the genre—is his nice sense of self-deprecation. We can take him seriously as a human being—because he doesn't take *himself* seriously.

A typical exchange between Marlowe and a disgruntled barman:

"Drink while waiting?"
    "A dry martini will do."
    "A martini. Dry. Veddy, veddy dry."
    "Okay."
    "Will you eat it with a spoon or a knife and fork?"
    "Cut it in strips," I said. "I'll just nibble it."
    "On your way to school," he said. "Should I put the olive in a bag for you?"
    "Sock me on the nose with it," I said. "If it will make you feel any better."
    "Thank you, sir," he said. "A dry martini."

                                        —*The High Window*

As Chandler said, he is "the sort of guy who behaves according to the company he is in":

He talks as the man of his age talks, that is, with rude wit, a lively sense of the grotesque, a disgust for sham, and a contempt for pettiness.

                                        —"The Simple Art of Murder"

The clichés of his business never cease to amuse him . . .

I rumpled my hair which was already rumpled. I put the old tired grin on my face.

—The Long Goodbye

"You can always tell a detective on TV. He never takes his hat off."

—Playback

The actual mechanics of smoking provide another Marlowe theme:

I killed my cigarette and got another one out and went through all the slow futile face-saving motions of lighting it, getting rid of the match, blowing smoke off to one side, inhaling deeply, as though that scrubby little office was a hilltop overlooking the bouncing ocean—all the tired clichéd mannerisms of my trade.

—The Little Sister

I sat down and lit a cigarette, the always mechanical reaction that gets so boring when someone else does it.

—Playback

I lit my pipe again. It makes you look thoughtful when you are not thinking.

—Farewell, My lovely

He lit his cigarette the way I do myself, missing twice on the thumbnail and then using his foot.

—The Big Sleep

I snicked a match on my thumbnail and for once it lit.

—The Big Sleep

Quite often he would use a large wooden "kitchen" match—or else his trusty Zippo lighter:

> You should be able to do it one-handed. You can, too, but it's an awkward process.
>
> —*Playback*

Then there's the technique of getting heavy with a heavy, or separating someone from a nasty-looking gun pointed in your direction . . .

> The idea was to get close enough to make a side swipe at the gun, knock it outwards and then jump in fast before she could bring it back in line. I've never had a lot of luck with the technique, but you have to try it once in a while.
>
> —*The Lady in the Lake*

> A kid trick, but once in a while it will work, especially after a lot of smart conversation, full of worldliness and sly wit.
>
> —*The High Window*

At least once in every story, however, it *doesn't* work and Marlowe is required to sleep the small poetic sleep. As the series hero, he clearly can't be killed, and yet, if he were to escape unscathed, he would rapidly lose all credibility. Therefore, he must take a beating or two. Interestingly, it is these episodes that seem to bring out the most purple and personal of Chandler's prose, and one is left with the feeling that the imagery of violence could apply equally well to a man on an alcoholic binge—something he knew a good deal about.

> There was nothing but hard aching white light, then there was darkness in which something red wriggled like a germ under a microscope, then there was nothing bright or wriggling, just darkness and emptiness and a rushing wind and a falling as of great trees.
>
> —*The Big Sleep*

A pool of darkness opened at my feet and was far, far deeper than the blackest night. I dived in. It had no bottom.

—*Farewell, My Lovely*

At that moment an army mule kicked me square on the back of my brain. I went zooming out over a dark sea and exploded in a sheet of flame.

—*Playback*

The scene exploded into fire and darkness . . . and just before the darkness a sharp flash of nausea.

—*The Lady in the Lake*

It had been happening to Marlowe for years . . .

The floor rose up and bumped me. I sat on it as on a raft in a rough sea . . . Drums were beating in my head now, war drums from a far-off jungle. Waves of light were moving, and dark shadows and a rustle as of a wind in the treetops. I didn't want to lie down. I lay down.

—"Goldfish"—1936

I was looking at the ceiling, lying on my back on the floor, a position in which my calling has occasionally placed me . . . I was as dizzy as a dervish, as weak as a worn-out washer, as low as a badger's belly, as timid as a titmouse, and as unlikely to succeed as a ballet dancer with a wooden leg.

—*The Little Sister*

. . . as, indeed, it had to his predecessors, such as Carmady ("Then all the lights went out very slowly, as in a theatre just as the curtain goes up"—"The Man Who Liked Dogs," 1936) ("I went out like a puff of dust in a draft"—"The Curtain," 1936) or John Dalmas ("My head was a large pink firework exploding into the vault of the sky and scattering and falling slow and pale, and then dark, into the waves. Blackness ate me up."—"Bay City Blues," 1938) or John Evans ("My head came off and went halfway across the lake and did a boomerang turn and came back and slammed on top of my spine with a sickening jar."—"No Crime in the Mountains," 1941) or Walter Gage ("I bent over and took hold of the room with both hands and spun it. When I had it nicely spinning I gave it a full swing and hit myself on the back of the head with the floor."—"Pearls Are a Nuisance," 1939).

After which comes the invariable hangover—and Chandler managed to find variations on that, too . . .

> It was my voice but somebody had been using my tongue for sandpaper . . . I was leaning against the bathroom wall and sorting out my fingers.
>
> —*The Little Sister*

> Blood was beginning to move around in me, like a prospective tenant looking over a house.
>
> —*The Big Sleep*

> I lifted a foot at last, dragged it out of the cement it was stuck in, took a step, and then hauled the other foot after it like a ball and chain.
>
> —"The Lady in the Lake"—short story, 1939

> It took a lot out of me, and there wasn't as much to spare as there once had been. The hard heavy years had worked me over.
>
> —*The Long Goodbye*

Humor is Marlowe's armor against the mean streets and grim ghettoes, but there are times when it deserts him and we find the "lonely man" in the lonely room that Chandler essentially saw him to be. Linda Loring taunts him in *The Long Goodbye*:

> "What have you now? An empty house to come home to, with not even a dog or cat, a small stuffy office to sit in and wait."
> I filled and lit my pipe and sat there smoking. Nobody came in, nobody called, nothing happened, nobody cared whether I died or went to El Paso.
>
> —*The High Window*

I looked at my watch. Nine forty-four. Time to go home and get your slippers on. Time for a tall cool drink and a long quiet pipe. Time to sit with your feet up and think of nothing. Time to start yawning over your magazine. Time to be a human being, a householder, a man with nothing to do but rest and suck in the night air and rebuild the brain for tomorrow.

—*The Lady in the Lake*

Having thought that, Marlowe goes off to walk another mean street . . .

I watched the last of the sunlight sneak over my windowsill and drop into the dark slit of the valley.

—"Bay City Blues"

Let the telephone ring, please. Let there be somebody to call up and plug me into the human race . . . Nobody has to like me. I just want to get off this frozen star.

—*The Little Sister*

Marlowe's dilemma is that he has no choice. For him it is this or nothing. In *The Long Goodbye* he contemplates the alternative that most people settle for—the American Dream of middle-class home and family:

You take it, friend. I'll take the big sordid dirty crooked city.

[Marlowe] is a lonely man and his pride is that you will treat him as a proud man or be very sorry you ever saw him.

—"The Simple Art of Murder"

After five Marlowe novels, Chandler had evolved his personal philosophy of what it took to be a private eye:

The detective exists complete and entire and unchanged by anything that happens; he is, as detective, outside the story and above it, and always will be. That is why he never gets the girl, never marries, never really has any private life except insofar as he must eat and sleep and have a place to keep his clothes. His moral and intellectual force is that he gets nothing but his fee, for which he will if he can protect the innocent, guard the helpless, and destroy the wicked, and the fact that he must do this while earning a meager living in a corrupt world is what makes him stand out. A rich idler has nothing to lose but his dignity; the professional is subject to all the pressures of an urban civilization and must rise above them to do his job. Because he represents justice and not the law, he will sometimes defy or break the law. Because he is human he can be hurt or beguiled or fooled; in extreme necessity he may even kill. But he does nothing solely for himself.

—Letter to James Sandoe—May 12, 1949

It's easy—especially today—to read all sorts of liberal values into Marlowe, but he was not one who saw himself as a knight errant. Merely a guy doing a job. It takes Chandler to remind us that he is a literary creation, not a real man: "The private detective of fiction is a fantastic creation, who acts and speaks like a real man."

When critics endlessly discussed Marlowe's "social conscience," Chandler became irritated. "Marlowe has as much social conscience as a horse. He has a *personal* conscience, which is an entirely different matter." And then the identification creeps in. "Philip Marlowe and I do not despise the upper classes because they take baths and have money; we despise them because they are phony" (Letter to Dale Warren—January 7, 1945).

> "It's no real fun but the rich don't know that. They never had any. They never want anything very hard except maybe somebody else's wife and that's a pretty pale desire compared with the way a plumber's wife wants new curtains for the living room."
>
> —*The Long Goodbye*

To hell with the rich. They made me sick.

> —*The Big Sleep*

And they weren't the only ones. When his sense of humor was on hold:

You can have a hangover from other things than alcohol. I had one from women. Women made me sick.

> —*The Big Sleep*

"You self-sufficient, self-satisfied, self-confident bastard."

> —Linda Loring in *The Long Goodbye*

"You're the hardest guy to get anything out of. You don't even move your ears."

> —Vivian Regan in *The Big Sleep*

All us tough guys are hopeless sentimentalists at heart.

> —Letter to Roger Machell—February 7, 1955

And when in 1957 toward the end of his life, Chandler talks about Marlowe being "a character of some nobility, of scorching wit, sad but not defeated, lonely but never really sure of himself," one is left wondering which of them he is *really* talking about.

For the problem with a fictional character—particularly the kind of emotional *doppelgänger* of Chandler that Marlowe had become—is that, as the writer ages and changes, so does the character, often in ways his creator is unaware of until they are pointed out.

Whether Chandler realized it or not, Marlowe had changed by *The Little Sister,* for the simple reason that Chandler himself had changed. His Hollywood experience had soured him and he had not enjoyed writing the book, even though it was to make him financially independent. It was, he said, "the only book of mine I have actively disliked. It was written in a bad mood and I think that comes through."

It certainly came through in Marlowe's self-evaluation:

A blank man. I had no face, no meaning, no personality, hardly a name. I didn't want to eat, I didn't even want a drink. I was a page from yesterday's calendar crumpled at the bottom of the waste basket . . .

There are days like that. Everybody you meet is a dope. You begin to look at yourself in the glass and wonder . . . Hold it, Marlowe, you're not human tonight.

Soon after writing this, Chandler expressed his concern to Hamish Hamilton (August 10, 1948):

The trouble with the Marlowe character is he has been written and talked about too much. He's getting self-conscious, trying too much to live up to his reputation among the quasi-intellectuals. The boy is bothered. He used to be able to spit and throw the ball hard and talk out of the side of his mouth.

He will at any time, because he is that sort of man, meet any danger, since he thinks that is what he was created for, and because he knows the corruption of his country can only be cured by men who are determined if necessary to sacrifice themselves to cure it. He doesn't talk or behave like an idealist, but I think he is one at heart; and I think that he rather hates to admit it, even to himself.

The Long Goodbye was a revelation to him. It was meant to break away from Marlowe. He wrote the first draft in the third person before he "realized I have absolutely no interest in the leading character. He was merely a name; so I'm afraid I'm going to have to start all over and hand the assignment to Mr. Marlowe . . . It begins to look as though I were tied to this fellow for life. I simply can't function without him," he wrote to his British publisher, Hamish Hamilton (July 14, 1951), with the kind of recognition of the inevitable that Conan Doyle never expressed in a comparable context about his own invention, Sherlock Holmes.

The situation was not exactly one that any writer would choose for his chef d'oeuvre . . .

I watched my wife die by half-inches and I wrote my best book in my agony of that knowledge. I don't know how. I used to shut myself in my study and think myself into another world. It usually took an hour, at least. And then I went to work.

—Letter to Jean de Leon—February 11, 1957

What he didn't realize was what the changes in him had done to Marlowe. From *The Long Goodbye*:

No feelings at all was exactly right. I was as hollow as the spaces between the stars.

I got home late and tired and depressed. It was one of those nights when the air is heavy and the night noises seem muffled and far away. There was a high misty and indifferent moon. I walked the floor, played a few records and hardly heard them. I seemed to hear a steady ticking somewhere, but there wasn't anything in the house to tick. The ticking was in my head, I was a one-man death watch.

"I don't mind Marlowe being a sentimentalist, because he always has been. His toughness has more or less always been a surface bluff," he wrote to Hamilton; but to Bernice Baumgarten he went further:

I knew the character of Marlowe had changed and I thought it had to because the hardboiled stuff was too much of a pose after all this time. But I did not realize that it had become Christ-like and sentimental, and that he ought to be deriding his own emotions.

Other characters in Marlowe's world did seem to recognize the changes in him—almost as though they could sense what Chandler could not.

It was always par for the course for his opponents to abuse him, verbally as well as physically, but in the early novels they do it as much out of fear of this one-man army as anything else. Their insults are reverse compliments.

Jules Amthor in *Farewell, My Lovely* calls him "a dirty little man in a dirty little world." But he was busy making it dirtier . . . But by *The Long Goodbye* Menendez, a second-rate hoodlum, feels able to insult him at length:

> "You're a piker, Marlowe. You're a peanut grifter. You're so little it takes a magnifying glass to see you . . . You've got cheap emotions. You're cheap all over . . . You got no guts, no brains, no connections, no savvy, so you throw out a phony attitude and expect people to cry over you. Tarzan on a big red scooter . . . In my book you're a nickel's worth of nothing."

Admittedly, Marlowe hits him in the stomach immediately after that speech—but Menendez wasn't the only one to be hurt.

Toward the end—and in the depths of his own misery after Cissy's death—Chandler lost control of both himself and his own creation, and appeared to realize it. Marlowe is tired and as near defeated as Chandler must have felt. ("I'm not a young man. I'm old, tired and full of no coffee.") At the end of *Playback* (1958)—quite out of the blue—he rather arbitrarily brings back Linda Loring and sets up the scenario for their reconciliation in the intended sequel, *Poodle Springs*. ("Hold me close in your arms. I don't want to own you. Nobody ever will. I just want to love you.")

But on reflection Chandler had his doubts:

> I am writing him married to a rich woman and swamped by money, but I don't think it will last . . . A fellow of Marlowe's type shouldn't get married, because he is a lonely man, a poor man, a dangerous man, and yet a sympathetic man, and somehow none of this goes with marriage.
> —Letter to Maurice Guinness—February 21, 1959

In this he was echoing his own earlier edict: "A really good detective never gets married. He would lose his detachment, and this detachment is part of his charm."

"I think the struggle between them," he wrote to Jessica Tyndale (December 23, 1957),

> as to whether he is going to live her kind of life or his own might make a good sub-plot. Either she will give in or the marriage will bust up. I don't know. But I do know that nobody, but nobody, is going to keep Marlowe from his shabby office and his unremunerative practice, his endurance, determination and his sarcastic pity. She'll probably want to redo his office but she won't get to first base on that either.

Chandler was almost certainly right—but we were never to know. His last thoughts were expressed in a letter to Maurice Guinness written a few days before he died.

> I think I may have picked the wrong girl. But as a matter of fact, a fellow of Marlowe's type shouldn't get married . . . I think he will always have . . . a number of affairs, but no permanent connection. I think he will always be awakened at some inconvenient hour by some inconvenient person, to do some inconvenient job. It seems to me that is his destiny—possibly not the best destiny in the world, but it belongs to him. No one will ever beat him, because by his nature he is unbeatable. No one will ever make him rich, because he is destined to be poor. But somehow, I think he would not have it otherwise . . . I see him always in a lonely street, in lonely rooms, puzzled but never quite defeated.

"I was a grain of sand on the desert of oblivion."
—The Long Goodbye

"It was the job—and that's all a guy can say."
—Mallory in "Smart-Aleck Kill"

Let's not go into that. You're not human tonight, Marlowe.
Maybe I never was or ever will be.
—The Little Sister

"I'm going the way I always go," I said. "With an airy smile and a quick flip of the wrist."

—*The High Window*

From time to time Marlowe would wonder how else he might have lived . . .

I would have stayed in the town where I was born and worked in the hardware store and married the boss's daughter and had five kids and read them the funny papers on Sunday morning and smacked their heads when they got out of line and squabbled with the wife about how much spending money they were to get and what program they could have on the radio or TV set. I might even have got rich—small-town rich, an eight-room house, two cars in the garage, chicken every Sunday and the *Reader's Digest* on the living-room table, the wife with a cast-iron permanent and me with a brain like a sack of Portland cement. You take it, friend. I'll take the big sordid dirty crooked city.

—*The Long Goodbye*

Four

Cops ... and Crime

"Cops are just people," she said irrelevantly.
 "They start out that way, I've heard. "

—*Farewell, My Lovely*

I never saw any of them again — except the cops. No way has yet been invented to say goodbye to them.

—*The Little Sister*

The hard stare they think they have to wear on their pans forever and forever and forever. I'm a cop, brother, I'm tough, watch your step, brother . . . let's go, and let's not forget we're tough guys, we're cops . . .

—*The Lady in the Lake*

"I think you need a good lawyer."

"That's a contradiction in terms," she sneered. "If he was good, he wouldn't be a lawyer."

—*Playback*

The law was something to be manipulated for profit and power. The streets were dark with something more than night.

—Introduction to *Trouble Is My Business*

"Organized crime is just the dirty side of the sharp dollar."

—*The Long Goodbye*

From early on in his voluntary Californian exile, Chandler was in little doubt as to the nature of the society he found there. He would speak of Marlowe's crusade as "the struggle of all fundamentally honest men to make a decent living in a corrupt society. It is an impossible struggle; he can't win." It was his own struggle, too—at least intellectually—to live in "this strange corrupt world" where "any man who tried to be honest looks in the end either sentimental or just plain foolish."

Toward the end of his life he saw it even more clearly:

I don't think one can accept or be happy with corrupt people without being a little corrupt oneself. It seems to me a sort of disease which grows almost unnoticed until one doesn't even know what is happening, and when it has happened, one doesn't know that either . . .

—Letter to Michael Gilbert—July 5, 1957

The one thing Raymond Chandler knew he could do was *write* about it, so that people would be made aware.

The underlying reasons for the decay were not hard to determine.

The introduction of Prohibition in 1920 was the start of open season for organized crime. Overnight ordinary citizens became "criminals" in the technical sense of the word, simply because they wanted a drink. The demand created the illegal supplier who, in turn, had to corrupt the local cops so that he could do business. That business rapidly became highly competitive, which led to gangsterism—and American society was bequeathed a *modus operandi* that persists to this day. But Chandler was there to see and document its emergence.

In the rotting social scene that he saw all about him, perhaps the most dangerous element was the enemy within. The cops.

In one of his many confrontations with L.A.'s finest, Marlowe expresses his (and Chandler's) essential philosophy of personal justice:

Prohibition—the Volstead Act (1920–1933). And the start of organized crime . . .

I said: "Until you guys own your own souls you don't own mine. Until you guys can be trusted every time and always, in all times and conditions, to seek the truth out and find it and let the chips fall where they may—until that time comes, I have a right to listen to my conscience, and protect my client the best way I can. Until I'm sure you won't do him more harm than you'll do the truth good."

He receives a predictably cynical answer from Lieutenant Breeze, the cop he's talking to . . .

"You sound to me just a little like a guy who is trying to hold his conscience down."

—*The High Window*

Captain Webber of Bay City is less emotional and more pragmatic about it when he tells Marlowe:

"Police business," he said almost gently, "is a hell of a problem. It's a good deal like politics. It asks for the highest type of men, and there's nothing in it to attract the highest type of men. So we have to work with what we get—and we get things like this."

"I know," I said. "I've always known that. I'm not bitter about it."

—*The Lady in the Lake*

"I just thought of what is the matter with policeman's dialogue."

"What?"

"They think every line is a punch line."

—*The High Window*

Policeman's dialogue. It comes out of an old shoe box. What they say doesn't mean anything. What they ask doesn't mean anything. They just keep on boring in until you are so exhausted that you flip on some detail.

—*"The Pencil"*

In *The Little Sister,* a cop, Lieutenant Christy-French, reminds Marlowe of what it is to be one . . .

"It's like this with us, baby. We're coppers and everybody hates our guts. And as if we didn't have enough trouble, we have to have you. As if we didn't get pushed around enough by the guys in the corner offices, the City Hall gang, the day chief, the night chief, the Chamber of Commerce, His Honor the Mayor in his paneled office four times as big as the three lousy rooms the whole homicide staff has to work out of. As if we didn't have enough to handle one hundred and fourteen homicides last year out of three rooms that don't have enough chairs for the whole duty squad to sit down in at once. We spend our lives turning over dirty underwear and sniffing rotten teeth. We go up dark stairways to get a gun punk with a skinful of hop and sometimes we don't get all the way up and our wives wait dinner that night and all the other nights. We don't come home any more. And nights we do come home, we come home so goddam tired we can't eat or sleep or even read the lies the papers print about us. So we lie awake in the dark in a cheap house in a cheap street and listen to the drunk down the block having fun. And just about the time we drop off the phone rings and we get up and start all over again. Nothing we do is right, not ever. Not once. If we get a confession, we beat it out of the guy, they say, and some shyster calls us Gestapo in court and sneers at us when we muddle our grammar. If we make a mistake they put us back in uniform on Skid Row and we spend the nice cool summer evenings picking drunks out of the gutter and being yelled at by whores and taking knives away from greaseballs in zoot suits. But all that ain't enough to make us entirely happy. We got to have you . . .

"We got to have you . . . We got to have sharpers with private licenses hiding information and dodging around corners and stirring up dust for us to breathe in. We got to have you suppressing evidence and framing set-ups that wouldn't fool a sick baby. You wouldn't mind me calling you a goddam cheap double-crossing keyhole peeper, would you, baby?"

". . . Some of what you say is true," I said. "Not all. Any private eye wants to play ball with the police. Sometimes it's a little hard to find out who's making the rules of the ball game. Sometimes he doesn't trust the police, and with cause. Sometimes he just gets into a jam without meaning to and has to play his hand the way it's dealt. He'd usually rather have a new deal. He'd like to keep on earning a living."

"They had the calm weathered faces of healthy men in hard condition. They had the eyes they always have, cloudy and gray like freezing water. The firm set mouth, the hard little wrinkles at the corners of the eyes, the hard hollow meaningless stare, not quite cruel and a thousand miles from kind. The dull ready-made clothes, worn without style, with a sort of contempt, the look of men who are poor and yet proud of their power, watching always for ways to make it felt, to shove it into you and twist it and grin and watch you squirm, ruthless without malice, cruel and yet not always unkind. What would you expect them to be? Civilization had no meaning for them. All they saw of it was the failures, the dirt, the dregs, the aberrations and the disgust."

—*The Little Sister*

By and large, in Chandler's perception the flawed triers like Christy-French are in the minority. His usual physical depiction of the police is not a flattering one:

Two uniformed cops barged into the room. They were the usual large size and they had the usual weathered faces and suspicious eyes.

—*The Lady in the Lake*

The usual couple in the usual suits, with the usual stony leisure of movement, as if the world was waiting hushed and silent for them to tell it what to do.

—*The Long Goodbye*

A police cruiser, c. 1950.

"We're a couple of swell guys not to get funny with."
                                        —*Trouble Is My Business*

"All tough guys are monotonous. Like playing cards with a deck that's all aces. You've got everything and you've got nothing."
                                        —*The Long Goodbye*

For example . . .

Chief Tod McKim ("Spanish Blood") "was a big, loose man who had gone saggy. He had a long, petulantly melancholy face. One of his eyes was not quite straight in his head."

Captain Gregory (*The Big Sleep*) is "a burly man with tired eyes and the slow deliberate movement of a night watchman. His voice was toneless, flat and uninterested."

Lieutenant Degarmo (*The Lady in the Lake*) is "the big cop with the dusty blond hair and the metallic blue eyes and the savage lined face"—who turns out to be a killer.

Captain Gregorius in *The Long Goodbye*: "a type of copper that is getting rarer but by no means extinct, the kind that solves crimes with the bright light, the soft sap, the kick to the kidneys, the knee to the groin, the night stick to the base of the spine."

Bay City's chief of police, John Wax, in *Farewell, My Lovely* is a much smoother proposition:

> He was a hammered down heavyweight with short pink hair and a pink scalp glistening through it. He has small, hungry, heavy-lidded eyes, as restless as fleas. He wore a suit of fawn-colored flannel, a coffee-colored shirt and tie, a diamond ring, a diamond-studded lodge pin in his lapel . . . He turned in his chair and crossed his thick legs . . . that let me see handspun lisle socks and English brogues that looked as if they had been pickled in port wine. Counting what I couldn't see and not counting his wallet, he had half a grand on him. I figured his wife had money.

More often than not, the eyes have it . . .

"His eyes were as blank as new plates" (*The Lady in the Lake*). Lieutenant Greer "sat down on the edge of a chair, the way they do . . . and looked at me with the quiet stare they have" (*The Lady in the Lake*). Sergeant Whitestone (*Poodle Springs*) had "the sort of eyes that every police sergeant gets in time. Eyes that have seen too much nastiness and heard too many liars." "That dead gray expression that grows on them like scum on a water tank" (*The Little Sister*).

Lieutenant Nulty (*Farewell, My Lovely*) is "a lean-jawed sourpuss with long yellow hands which he kept folded over his kneecaps." But at least Nulty has some redeeming features. "His shirt was frayed and his coat sleeves had been turned in at the cuffs. He looked poor enough to be honest."

But, like a lot of the cops Marlowe encounters, Nulty is a racist and a bigot—tags that some critics have tried to hang on Marlowe himself. The fact of the matter is that much of Marlowe's conversation is banter—sometimes lighthearted but more often, where cops are concerned, a defensive fencing. When the other person lowers the level of debate, then Marlowe is involved by association; for, as Chandler said, he wanted his hero to talk "as a man of his age talks . . . with a rude wit, a lively sense of the grotesque, a disgust for sham and a contempt for pettiness." And while Marlowe did not agree with the context of the banter, it would have been unrealistic of him not to understand and use the street language of a man like Nulty . . .

Shines. Another shine killing. That's what I rate after eighteen years in this man's police department. No pix, no space, not even four lines in the want-ad section.

The night captain . . . is tired and cynical and competent. He is the stage manager of a play that has had the longest run in history, but it no longer interests him.

—*The Long Goodbye*

"He was the kind of cop who spits on his blackjack every night instead of saying his prayers," Marlowe observes of one in *Farewell, My Lovely*. "But he had humorous eyes."

In many cases the coarseness is self-protection. In *The Big Sleep* Gregory tells Marlowe . . .

"I'm a copper. Just a plain ordinary copper. Reasonably honest. As honest as you could expect a man to be in a world where it's out of style . . . Being a copper I like to see the law win . . . you and me both lived too long to think I'm likely to see it happen. Not in this town, not in any town half this size, in any part of this wide, green and beautiful USA. We just don't run our country that way."

"He didn't know the right people. That's all a police record means in this rotten crime-ridden country."

—*The Big Sleep*

But—as Chandler decreed—"Marlowe wouldn't be Marlowe if he could really get along with policemen."

In the years he lived in Southern California, Chandler watched and deplored the twin pollution of the climate and the culture. And the bigger Los Angeles grew, the uglier it got, as organized crime moved in on the locals.

In *The Big Sleep* Marlowe has a word to the wise for local big shot Eddie Mars . . .

"This is a big town now, Eddie. Some very rough people have checked in here lately. The penalty of growth."

Maybe Eddie should move his business down the coast a piece to somewhere like Bay City (Chandler's wafer-thin alias for Santa Monica) . . .

> "Bay City. The name's like a song. A song in a dirty bathtub."
> —*Farewell, My Lovely*

> "But you can only buy a piece of a big city. You can buy a town this size all complete, with the original box and tissue paper. That's the difference."
> —*Farewell, My Lovely*

Money—Chandler felt—really was the root of most of the evil. The American psyche was obsessed with the almighty dollar. In *The Long Goodbye* Marlowe tells Bernie Ohls . . .

> "We're a big, rough, rich wild people and crime is the price we pay for it, and organized crime is the price we pay for organization. We'll have it with us a long time. Organized crime is just the dirty side of the sharp dollar."
> "As for the top men . . . they didn't get there by murdering people. They got there by guts and brains . . . But above all they're businessmen. What they do is for money. Just like other businessmen. Sometimes a guy gets in the way. Okay. Out. But they think plenty before they do it."
> —*The Long Goodbye*

In *Farewell, My Lovely* the cop "Hemingway" had expressed the same thought rather more colloquially:

> "Listen, pally . . . Cops don't go crooked for money. Not always, not even often. They get caught in the system. They get you where they have you do what is told them or else . . . A guy can't stay honest if he wants to. That's what's the matter with this country. He gets chiseled out of his pants if he does. You gotta play the game dirty or you don't eat."

Later Marlowe mulls it all over . . .

I thought of cops, tough cops that could be greased and yet were not by any means all bad . . . Fat prosperous cops with the Chamber of Commerce voices . . . Slim, smart and deadly cops . . . who for all their smartness and deadlines were not free to do a clean job in a clean way.

And D.A. Sewell Endicott puts his finger on another problem:

"The citizen is the law. In this country we haven't got around to understanding that. We think of the law as an enemy. We're a nation of cop-haters."

—*The Little Sister*

A district attorney may be the top honcho in the police hierarchy, but Marlowe is in no doubt about his inevitable angle: he wants to be famous.

"He eats publicity like I eat tender young garden peas," the cop Beifus tells Marlowe in *The Little Sister,* while in *The Long Goodbye* the current incumbent is running true to form—"The D.A. smells a lot of headlines on this one."

By this time Endicott is no longer D.A. but back in private practice. His view of the law remains cynical . . .

"The law isn't justice. It's a very imperfect mechanism. If you press exactly the right buttons and are also lucky, justice may show up in the answer. A mechanism is all the law was ever intended to be."

Years of exposure to L.A.'s finest had also given Marlowe a somewhat questioning attitude. By and large he (and Chandler) felt they were "a pretty dumb bunch who operate on the mental level of plumbers."

"There's no law against lying to the cops. They expect it. They feel much happier when you lie to them than when you refuse to talk to them. That's a direct challenge to their authority."

—*The Long Goodbye*

All the simple old-fashioned charm of a cop beating up a drunk.

You don't shake hands with big city cops. That close is too close.

—The Long Goodbye

"What makes you Bay City cops so tough? . . . You pickle your nuts in salt water or something?"

—The Little Sister

I smelled his sweat and the gas of corruption.

—The Long Goodbye

He leaned back and hooked his thumbs in his vest, which made him look a little more like a cop.

—Farewell, My Lovely

His blue uniform coat fitted him the way a stall fits a horse.

—"Bay City Blues"

"Or maybe we walk ourselves into some hot lead."

"Just like the coppers do on the radio," I said.

—"Bay City Blues"

"I'm just one of those sadistic cops that has to smack a head with a piece of lead pipe every so often to keep from getting nervous indigestion."

—"Bay City Blues"

"Oh, Christ, a sensitive cop!"

—Farewell, My Lovely

But when all is said and done . . .

I replaced the phone thinking that an honest cop with a bad conscience always acts tough. So does a dishonest one. So does almost anyone, including me.

—The Long Goodbye

So, were there no good cops?

Well, there was Lieutenant Carl Randall from Central Homicide in *Farewell, My Lovely*—"a thin, quiet man of fifty with smooth creamy gray hair, cold eyes, a distant manner"—who had, in Marlowe's opinion, "a lot behind his vest besides his shirt."

Randall warns Marlowe:

"Little by little you will build up a body of hostility in this department that will make it damned hard for you to do any work."

"Every private dick faces that every day of his life."

There was Lieutenant Breeze in *The High Window*:

The only thing about him which very much suggested cop was the calm, unwinking, unwavering stare of his prominent pale blue eyes, a stare that had no thought of being rude but that anybody but a cop would feel to be rude.

And then there was the deceptively rustic Sheriff Patton in *The Lady in the Lake,* running for reelection on the slogan "Keep Jim Patton Constable. He is too old to go to work."

He had a sweat-stained Stetson on the back of his head and his large hairless hands were clasped comfortably over his stomach . . . His hair was mousy brown except at the temples, where it was the color of old snow . . . He had large ears and friendly eyes and his jaws munched slowly and he looked as dangerous as a squirrel and much less nervous.

And then, of course, there was Bernie Ohls, "white eyebrows and an out-thrust, very deeply cleft chin" ("Finger Man"); "a medium-sized blondish man with stiff white eyebrows, calm eyes and well kept teeth. He looked like anybody you would pass on the streets. I happened to know that he had killed nine men" (*The Big Sleep*).

In several of the novels Ohls is Marlowe's *alter ego*—a cop who is tough but basically honest and realistic about this flawed paradise they share. Ohls speaks for both of them when he says, "There ain't no clean way to make a million bucks. The difference between him and most of the other cops is that he is prepared to clean up the dirt, instead of regarding it as inevitable and wallowing in it."

"I don't like hoodlums."

"That's just a word, Marlowe. We have that kind of world. Two wars gave it to us and we are going to keep it."

—*The Long Goodbye*

"That's the difference between crime and business. For business you gotta have capital. Sometimes I think it's the only difference."

"A properly cynical remark," I said, "but big time crime takes capital, too!"

"And where does it come from, chum? Not from guys that hold up liquor stores."

—*The Long Goodbye*

In "The Pencil" Ohls tells Marlowe:

"This town is getting to be almost as lousy as New York, Brooklyn or Chicago. We could end up real corrupt."

"We've made a hell of a good start."

He was frequently struck by—

"The strange psychological and spiritual kinship between the operations of big money business and the rackets. Same faces, same expressions, same manners . . . These boys all have good business fronts and very clever, although crooked, lawyers. Stop the lawyers and you stop the Syndicate, but the Bar Associations are simply not interested.

—Letter to Helga Greene—October 1, 1958

In "The Pencil" Marlowe tells Anne Riordan about the Mafia—

". . . the Outfit, the Syndicate, the big mob, or whatever name you want to use for it. You know damn well it exists and is as rich as Rockefeller. You can't beat it because not enough people want to, especially the million-a-year lawyers that work for it, and the bar associations that seem more anxious to protect other lawyers than their own country."

"My God, are you running for office somewhere? I never knew you sound so pure."

The image of the dollar is ever present in the world according to Chandler, and one of the things that unites Marlowe with Ohls and the occasional good cop who crosses his path is the clear-eyed realization that—in one way or another—everyone is out there looking for it.

On his way home from a case in *The Little Sister* Marlowe stops at a bar for a brandy. As he leaves:

I stepped out into the night air that nobody had yet found out how to option. But a lot of people were probably trying. They'd get around to it.

Five

The City of the Angels

Scattered diamond points at first, the lights drew together and became a jeweled wristlet laid out in the show window of the night.

— "The Man Who Liked Dogs"

"Everything's for sale in California."

—*The Lady in the Lake*

"We make the finest packages in the world, Mr. Marlowe. The stuff inside it is mostly junk."

—Harlan Potter in *The Long Goodbye*

"A big hard-boiled city with no more personality than a paper cup."

"It is the same in all big cities, amigo."

—*The Little Sister*

I smelled Los Angeles before I got to it. It smelled stale and old like a living room that had been closed too long. But the colored light fooled you.

—*The Little Sister*

———

Crime writer Ross Macdonald—considered by many to be the leading neo-Chandler—wrote that Chandler "invested the sun-blinded streets of Los Angeles with a romantic presence." But the romance was strictly of the film noir variety.

It was a time when the city was trying to carve out an identity for

Ross Macdonald (a.k.a. Kenneth Millar) (1915–1983). Now generally considered one of "the holy trinity of the American hard-boiled detective novel" with Hammett and Chandler. He named his detective, Lew Archer, as an homage to Hammett's Miles Archer, Sam Spade's murdered partner. He said that Chandler wrote "like a slumming angel . . . and invested the sun-blinded streets of Los Angeles with a romantic presence."
Alfred A. Knopf

itself. There are those who will tell you it still is. Hollywood was not the whole of Los Angeles; but in a very unreal sense, all of Los Angeles was Hollywood.

Architectural imagination ran riot. French *châteaux* sat cheek by jowl with Tudor castles and Italian villas. You might go to a restaurant like the Brown Derby, built to resemble a hat, or a bank that resembled an animal. A bottling plant a block long might have the exterior of an ocean liner with portholes for windows; a cinema posed as a Chinese pagoda—and still does. Everything was made to look like something else, and nothing seemed built to last—just like the film sets over in Hollywood.

There was money aplenty . . .

> There were great silent estates, with twelve-foot walls and wrought-iron gates and ornamental hedges; and inside, if you could get inside, a special brand of sunshine, very quiet, put up in noise-proof containers just for the upper classes.
>
> —*Farewell, My Lovely*

> The bright gardens had a haunted look, as though wild eyes were watching . . . from behind the bushes, as though the sunshine itself had a mysterious something in the light.
>
> —*The Big Sleep*

The house itself was not so much. It was smaller than Buckingham Palace, rather gray for California, and probably had fewer windows than the Chrysler Building . . . A man in a striped vest and gilt buttons opened the door, bowed, took my hat and was through for the day.

—*Farewell, My Lovely*

Inside the houses—were you privileged enough to get a peep—you were likely to find

the kind of room where people sit on floor cushions with their feet in their laps and sip absinthe through lumps of sugar and talk from the back of their throats in high, affected voices, and some of them just squeak. It was a room where anything could happen except work.

—*Farewell, My Lovely*

On the floor might be "a rug as thin as silk and as old as Aesop's aunt" ("Mandarin's Jade") or, alternatively, "You could just man-

Grauman's Chinese Theatre, 6931 Hollywood Boulevard. A movie theater posed as a Chinese pagoda—and still does. Everything was made to look like something else.
Photofest

The house in which Chandler had Joe Brody ("the two-bit chiseler") murdered in
The Big Sleep.

Wilshire Boulevard, 1935. Photofest

age to walk on the carpet without waders" (*The High Window*). "A peach-colored Chinese rug a gopher could have spent a week in without showing his nose above the nap" ("Mandarin's Jade").

When the old-money moment was past, the glow faded fast. The color scheme of the old Chateau Berry was

> bile green, linseed-poultice brown, sidewalk gray and monkey-bottom blue. It was as restful as a split lip.
>
> —*The Little Sister*

Raymond Chandler, one gathers, did not approve of the filthy rich, if only because of what they did with their money.

Chandler remembered the city as being "hot and dry when I first went there, with tropical rains in winter and sunshine at least nine-tenths of the year."

Hollywood Boulevard, 1937. Marlowe had his office at the mythical Cahuenga Building near Ivar—first on the seventh floor, then Suite 615. Photofest

The original Brown Derby restaurant was on Wilshire opposite the Ambassador Hotel. A second Brown Derby opened on North Vine Street in 1928 in the heart of Hollywood and attracted the top movie stars. Photofest

Marlowe also has his memories . . .

"I used to like this town," I said . . . "A long time ago. There were trees along Wilshire Boulevard. Beverly Hills was a country town. Westwood was bare hills and lots offering at eleven hundred dollars and no takers. Hollywood was a bunch of frame houses on the interurban line. Los Angeles was just a big dry sunny place with ugly homes and no style, but goodhearted and peaceful. It had the climate they just yap about now. People used to sleep out on porches. Little groups who thought they were intellectual used to call it the Athens of America. It wasn't that, but it wasn't a neon-lighted slum either."

—*The Little Sister*

It was a very different Los Angeles in those days. The 1911 Census had estimated 350,000 people but the trickle of immigrants was becoming a flood. By 1930 it would be 1.5 million and a lot of things would have changed.

An oil boom of massive proportions was under way, creating money and jobs—and it didn't much care for whom. Money poured into the state with the encouragement of the federal government. Before long the economy was that of a fair-sized country, and since it was easy money, it easily attracted organized crime.

World War II aggravated the situation. The setting-up of factories

Vine Street, 1953. Known for its famous restaurants such as the Brown Derby, nightclubs, high-end stores and theaters that broadcast live radio shows. Photofest

City Hall (which appears in The Little Sister *and other stories) and its neighbor,*
Union Station. Photofest

for arms manufacturing made California the epicenter of the defense
industry, and Washington—anxious to help rebuild the region after the
Depression of the 1930s—gave preference in the granting of contracts.

And still people poured in. By the 1950s the city boasted an elec-
tronic sign that showed the population increase minute-by-minute.
What it did not show was the range of problems that unplanned
influx brought with it.

It was all too much too soon for a town that had no evolved culture
of its own. What had emerged, Chandler saw as being just as much
the product of bland mass production and advertising. He called it
the "culture of the filter-tipped cigarette . . . leading to a steakless
steak to be broiled on a heatless broiler in a non-existent oven and
eaten by a toothless ghost."

In the books Marlowe is constantly crisscrossing the terrain, noting the morphing of one aspect into another—rarely for the better—and always making us aware of the geographical context in which this amorphous new "Athens" exists. Behind it, the timeless range of mountains. Before it, "the great fat solid Pacific trudging into shore like a scrubwoman going home . . . a California ocean. California, the department store state. The most of everything and the best of nothing" (*The Little Sister*). "There is a touch of the desert about everything in California and about the minds of the people who live here" (Letter to Blanche Knopf). We are constantly being made aware of natural beauty corrupted by unnatural man.

In a more mellow mood, the sea takes on more romantic imagery . . .

> Under the thinning fog the surf curled and creamed, almost without sound, like a thought trying to form itself on the edge of consciousness.
>
> —*The Big Sleep*

> The swell is as gentle as an old lady singing hymns.
>
> —*The Long Goodbye*

> In the cove the waves don't break, they slide in politely, like floor walkers.
>
> —*Playback*

In that mood the city itself has its own kind of beauty, though the imagery is invariably man-made: "The lights of the city were a vast golden carpet, stitched with brilliant splashes of red and green and blue and purple" ("Pick-Up on Noon Street") . . . "The lights of Hollywood and L.A. winked at him. Searchlight beams probed the cloudless sky as if searching for bombing planes" ("The King in Yellow") . . . "the stars were as bright and artificial as stars of chromium on a sky of black velvet" (*Farewell, My Lovely*) . . . "a slanting grey rain like a swung curtain of crystal beads" (*The Big Sleep*) . . . "The light hit pencils of rain and made silver wires of them" ("The Curtain") . . .

The valley moonlight was so sharp that the black shadows looked as though they had been cut with an engraving tool . . . ten thousand lighted windows and the stars hanging down over them politely, not getting too close.

—The High Window

The Beverly Hills Hotel was built in 1912 and immediately proved to be a magnet for the film community. Especially popular was the Polo Lounge, the pool and the private bungalows for rent. In the 1940s it was repainted in pink and green and acquired the nickname "the Pink Palace." Photofest

There was loneliness and the smell of kelp and the smell of wild sage from the hills. A yellow window hung here and there, all by itself, like the last orange.

—*Farewell, My Lovely*

Spring rustling in the air like a paper bag blowing along a concrete sidewalk.

—*Farewell, My Lovely*

We curved through the bright mile or two of the Sunset Strip past the antique shops with famous screen names on them, past the windows full of point lace and ancient pewter, past the gleaming new nightclubs with famous chefs and equally famous gambling rooms, run by polished graduates of the Purple Gang, past the Georgian Colonial vogue, now old hat, past the handsome modernistic buildings in which the Hollywood flesh-peddlers never stop talking money, past a drive-in lunch which somehow didn't belong, even though the girls wore white silk blouses and drum majorettes' shakos and nothing below the hips but glazed Hessian boots. Past all this and down a wide smooth curve to the bridle path of Beverly Hills and lights to the south, all colors of the spectrum and crystal clear in an evening without fog, past the shadowed mansions up on the hills to the north, past Beverly Hills altogether and up into the twisting foothill boulevard and the sudden cool dusk and the drift of wind from the sea.

—*Farewell, My Lovely*

"Beverly Hills was such a nice place before the Phoenicians took it over. Now it's just a setting for an enormous confidence racket."

As time—and Marlowe—go by, another incidental dimension emerges in Chandler's panorama of the city. Not only is it growing before our eyes but we are made aware of proximity. The bad and the beautiful exist literally cheek by jowl. Two blocks from obscene

1955. The 146-foot Richfield Building. "The lights were wonderful. There ought to be a monument to the man who invented neon lights. . . . There's a boy who really made something out of nothing" (The Little Sister).

wealth is abject poverty. The dreams of Hollywood coexist happily with the worst urban nightmares . . . and nobody seems to notice or care too much.

Even Nature is not to be trusted. It's always lying in wait for you . . .

There was a desert wind blowing that night. It was one of those dry Santa Anas that come down through the mountain passes and curl your hair and make your nerves jump and your skin itch. On nights like that every booze party ends in a fight. Meek little wives feel the edge of the carving knife and study their husband's necks. Anything can happen. You can even get a full glass of beer at a cocktail lounge.

—"Red Wind"

In *Farewell, My Lovely* the poetry is still present but it soon begins to sour.

They went through the silent streets, past blurred houses, blurred trees, the blurred shine of street lights. There were neon signs behind thick curtains of mist. There was no sky.

—"Pick-Up on Noon Street"

The colored lights fooled you. The lights were wonderful. There ought to be a monument to the man who invented neon lights. Fifteen stories high, solid marble. There's a boy who really made something out of nothing.

—*The Little Sister*

Bunker Hill. The Victorian-style houses are deceptive. By the 1940s this once exclusive district had seen its former grandeur transformed into rooming houses. "Bunker Hill is old town, lost town, shabby town, crook town. Once, very long ago, it was the choice residential district of the city" (The High Window).

The city was changing before Chandler's eyes, and the details become clearer with the passing years.

In "The King in Yellow" (1938):

Court Street was old town, wop town, crook town, arty town. It lay across the top of Bunker Hill and you could find anything there from down-at-the-heels ex–Greenwich Villagers to crooks on the lam, from ladies of anybody's evening to County Relief clients brawling with haggard landladies in grand old houses with scrolled porches, parquetry floors, and immense sweeping banisters of white oak, mahogany and Circassian walnut.

By *The High Window* (1942) the decay has become terminal:

Bunker Hill is old town, lost town, shabby town, crook town. Once, very long ago, it was the choice residential district of the city, and there are still standing a few of the jigsaw Gothic mansions with wide porches and walls covered with round-end shingles and full corner bay windows with spindle turrets. They are all rooming houses now, their parquetry floors are scratched and worn through the once glossy finish and the wide sweeping staircases are dark with time and with cheap varnish laid on over generations of dirt. In the tall rooms haggard landladies bicker with shifty tenants. On the wide cool front porches, reaching their cracked shoes into the sun and staring at nothing, sit the old men with faces like lost battles.

In and around the old houses there are flyblown restaurants and Italian fruit-stands and cheap apartment houses and little candy stores where you can buy even nastier things than their candy. And there are ratty hotels where nobody except people named Smith and Jones sign the register and where the night clerk is half watchdog and half pander.

Out of the apartment houses come women who should be young but have faces like stale beer, men with pulled-down hats and quick eyes that look the street over behind the cupped hand that shields the match flame; worn intellectuals with cigarette coughs and no money in the bank; fly cops with granite faces and unwavering eyes; cokies and coke peddlers; people who look like nothing in particular and know it.

Once in a while even men that actually go to work come out. But they come out early, when the wide cracked sidewalks are empty and still have dew on them.

The sadness for Chandler/Marlowe is how fast this has all happened to what is, by any definition, a "new" city . . .

I could see the Hotel Tremaine's sign over a narrow door between two store fronts, both empty—an old two-story walk-up. Its woodwork would smell of kerosene, its shades would be cracked, its curtains would be a sleazy cotton lace and its bedsprings would stick in your back. I knew all about places like the Hotel Tremaine. I had slept in them, staked out in them, fought with bitter, scrawny landladies in them, got shot at in them, and might yet get carried out of one of them to the morgue wagon. They are flops where you find the cheap ones, the sniffers and pin-jabbers, the gowed-up runts who shoot you before you can say hello.

—"Mandarin's Jade"

In *The Little Sister* (1948) there was the Van Nuys Hotel:

The memories of old cigars clung to its lobby like the dirty gilt on its ceiling . . . The corridor had a smell of old carpet and furniture oil and the drab anonymity of a thousand shabby lives.

Admittedly, twelve years before there had already been "blocks where silent men sat on shaky front porches and blocks where noisy young toughs of both colors snarled and wisecracked at one another in front of cheap restaurants and drugstores and beer parlors full of slot machines." And dives where "they look as if they only existed after dark, like ghouls. The people are dissipated without grace, sinful without irony" ("Blackmailers Don't Shoot").

The image of old people on decaying porches had stayed with him from his Nebraska days. It crops up again in *The Little Sister.* There they sit on their "wood and cane rockers . . . held together with wire and the moisture of the beach air."

The physical changes Chandler chronicled merely reflected the sociological ebb and flow, which were happening faster in Los Angeles than elsewhere in America. As more and more people poured in and the city became full to overflowing, the rich moved to less populated areas. The poor took over the vacated neighborhoods, changing the character of those environments overnight.

At the beginning of *Farewell, My Lovely* Marlowe refers to "one of those blocks over on Central Avenue, the blocks that are not yet all negro." Had Chandler lived, he would have seen a series of succeeding waves of which the Negro was simply the first. As many of them became "upwardly mobile," they were being pushed in turn by the New Poor from Asia and Latin America. All Chandler saw was the way relatively new developments were turned into instant slums, as the "white trash" areas turned black.

Society was volatile and social values in flux. In the same book Moose Malloy, looking for his onetime girlfriend, Velma, comes to the bar where she used to work. But Moose has been in prison for the last eight years and the bar is now a "dinge joint." There is a little difference of opinion, which leads to Moose killing or incapacitating three of the inhabitants. When questioned by the cops about what happened, Marlowe—who had been Moose's reluctant companion on the visit in question—answers ironically:

"Well, all he did was kill a negro . . . I guess that's only a misdemeanor."

By *Farewell, My Lovely* (1940) a spray-painted veneer is in place to hide all that, and in *The Little Sister* (1948) it's dried to a hard shine:

"We crossed La Cienega and went into the curve of the Strip. The Dancers was a blaze of light. The terrace was packed. The parking lot was like ants on a piece of overripe fruit.

The art deco Sunset Tower on Sunset Boulevard mentioned in The Big Sleep.

". . . We've got the big money, the sharp shooters, the percentage workers, the fast-dollar boys, the hoodlums out of New York and Chicago and Detroit—and Cleveland. We've got the flash restaurants and night clubs they run, and the hotels and apartment houses they own, and the grifters and con men and female handits that live in them. The luxury trades, the pansy decorators, the Lesbian dress designers, the riffraff of a big hard boiled city with no more personality than a paper cup.

Out in the fancy suburbs dear old Dad is reading the sports page in front of a picture window, with his shoes off, thinking he is high class because he has a three-car garage. Mom is in front of her princess dresser trying to paint the suitcases out from under her eyes. And Junior is clamped onto the telephone calling up a succession of high school girls that talk pigeon English and carry contraceptives in their make-up kit."

"It is the same in all big cities, amigo."

Later in the same story Marlowe takes another drive in what has become a numb commute for so many of his fellow citizens . . .

I drove east on Sunset but I didn't go home. At La Brea I turned north and swung over to Highland, out over Cahuenga Pass and down on to Ventura Boulevard, past Studio City and Sherman Oaks and Encino. There was nothing lonely about the trip. There never is on that road. Fast boys in stripped-down Fords shot in and out of the traffic streams, missing fenders by a sixteenth of an inch, but somehow always missing them. Tired men in dusty coupés and sedans winced and tightened their grip on the wheel and ploughed on north and west towards home and dinner, an evening with the sports page, the blatting of the radio, the whining of their spoiled children and the gabble of their silly wives. I drove on past the gaudy neons and the false fronts behind them, the sleazy hamburger joints that look like palaces under the colors. The circular drive-ins as gay as circuses with the chipper hard-eyed carhops, the brilliant counters, and the sweaty greasy kitchens that would have poisoned a toad. Great double trucks rumbled down over Sepulveda from Wilmington and San Pedro and crossed towards the Ridge Route, starting up in low-low from the traffic lights with a growl of lions in the zoo.

Landscape and locations become as real as characters.

The rot that Chandler detects is not confined to Los Angeles. As Marlowe and his clones go about their business we get to see that smaller neighboring communities are equally infected.

There's Bay City—his pseudonym for Santa Monica, where Chan-

"Bay City [Santa Monica] was a very nice place. People lived there and thought so . . . the nice blue bay and the cliffs . . . and the quiet streets of houses" (The Lady in the Lake). *Marlowe didn't agree: "All I know about Bay City is that every time I go there I have to buy a new head"* (The Little Sister).

dler and Cissy lived for five years ("Law is where you buy it in this town"—*Farewell, My Lovely*).

> Bay City was a very nice place. People lived there and thought so . . . the nice blue bay and the cliffs and the yacht harbor and the quiet streets of houses, old houses brooding under old trees and new houses with sharp green lawns and wire fences and staked saplings set into the parkway in front of them.
>
> —*The Lady in the Lake*

But appearances were often deceptive. Literally on the other side of the tracks:

> The Mexican and Negro slums stretched out on the dismal flats south of the old interurban tracks. Nor of the waterfront dives

along the flat shore south of the cliffs, the sweaty little dance halls on the pike, the marijuana joints, the narrow fox faces watching over the tops of newspapers in far too quiet hotel lobbies, nor the pickpockets and grifters and con men and drunk rollers and pimps and queens on the board walk.

—The Lady in the Lake

And on the Promenade:

Outside the narrow street fumed, the sidewalks swarmed with fat stomachs. Across the street a bingo parlor was going full blast and beside it a couple of sailors with girls were coming out of a photographer's shop . . . The voice of the hot dog merchant split the dusk like an axe . . . there was a faint smell of ocean. Not very much, but as if they had kept this much just to remind people this had once been a clean open beach where the waves came in and creamed and the wind blew and you could smell something besides the hot fat and cold sweat . . . beyond the smell of hot fat and popcorn and the shrill children and the barkers in the peepshows.

—Farewell, My Lovely

Later Chandler would remark that "a real clinical study of such a town would be fascinating reading."

As early as 1939 Chandler had seen the writing on the wall for the city and didn't like what he read one little bit. In a letter to fellow thriller writer George Harmon Coxe (October 17) he prophesied:

No doubt in years, or centuries to come, this will be the center of civilization, if there is any left, but the melting-pot stage bores me horribly. I like people with manners, grace, some social intuition, an education slightly above the *Reader's Digest* fan, people whose pride of living does not express itself in their kitchen gadgets and their automobiles . . . I like a conservative atmosphere, a sense of the past. I like everything that Americans of past generations used to go and look for in Europe, but at the same time I don't want to be bound by the rules.

For a while he and Cissy found refuge in La Jolla, a hundred miles south.

It has that intangible air of good breeding, which one imagines may still exist in New England, but which certainly does not exist any more in or around Los Angeles.

It had, he said,

the finest coastline of the Pacific side of the country, no billboards or concessions or beachfront shacks, an air of cool decency and good manners that is almost startling in California. One may like a free and easy neighborhood where they smash the empty bottles on the sidewalk. But in practice it's very comfortable.

Chandler's house at 6005 Camino de la Costa, La Jolla, California. "I like La Jolla, but La Jolla is only a sort of escape from reality . . . No doubt in years, or centuries to come, this will be the center of civilization, if there is any left." The Chandlers lived, left and returned several times in the itinerant 1940s and '50s.

"Now it is humid, hot and sticky, and when the smog comes down into the bowl between the mountains . . . it is damn near intolerable" (The Long Goodbye).
Photofest

But—as he admits to Coxe—

La Jolla is only a sort of escape from reality. It's not typical.

It would be an escape for the Chandlers for several years to come, and somehow it made the gritty reality of L.A. harder to take. The language becomes increasingly bitter:

I smelled Los Angeles before I got to it. It smelled stale and old like a living room that had been closed too long.

—The Little Sister

"I don't know what's happened to the weather in our overcrowded city," says Marlowe in "The Pencil." "But it's not the same weather I knew when I came to it."

Omnipresent, it seems—like the dust on Marlowe's desk—is the smog, the ironic result of California's perpetual sunshine interacting with that twentieth-century by-product, automobile emissions.

> The war has made it an individual city, and the climate has been ruined partly by this and partly by too much vegetation, too many lawns to be watered, and in a place that nature intended to be a semi-desert . . . Now it is humid, hot and sticky, and when the smog comes down into the bowl between the mountains which is L.A., it is damn near intolerable.
>
> —Letter to Helga Greene—May 7, 1957

> The weather was hot and sticky and the acid sting of the smog had crept as far west as Beverly Hills. From the top of Mulholland Drive you could see it leveled out all over the city like a ground mist and it made your eyes smart . . . Everything was the fault of the smog. If the canary wouldn't sing, if the milkman was late, if the Pekinese had fleas, if an old coot in a starched collar had a heart attack on the way to church, that was the smog.
>
> —*The Long Goodbye*

It was the metaphor for what was happening to his city and to him.

"I know what is the matter with my writing or not writing. I've lost any affinity for my background. Los Angeles is no longer my city," he wrote to Jessica Tyndale and to Hamish Hamilton—

> I have lost Los Angeles. It is no longer the place I knew so well and was almost the first to put on paper. I have that feeling, not very unusual, that I helped create the town and was then pushed out of it by the operators. I can hardly find my way around any longer.
>
> I know damn well I sound like a bitter and disappointed man. I guess I am at that.

In *The Long Goodbye* Marlowe sums up his city: "When I got home I mixed a stiff one and stood by the open window in the living room and sipped it." He looks out over "a city no worse than others, a city rich and vigorous and full of pride, a city lost and beaten and full of emptiness. It all depends on where you sit and what your own private score is. I didn't have one. I didn't care."

When the place of infinite possibilities becomes impossible, a man is entitled to be disappointed.

"I finished the drink and went to bed."

Six

Hollywood

The Hollywood sign started life as an advertising gimmick. Built in 1923, it cost $21,000. The letters were fifty feet tall and thirty feet wide. The LAND *was subsequently eliminated.*

Anyone who doesn't love Hollywood is either crazy or sober.
—Raymond Chandler

A preoccupation with words for their own sake is fatal to good film making. It's not what films are for.
—Letter to Dale Warren—November 7, 1951

It is much more difficult to write screenplays than novels. But it does not, in my opinion, take the same quality of talent. It may take a more exacting use of the talent, a more beautiful job of cabinet work, a finer or more apt ear for the current jargon of a certain kind of people, but it is much more superficial all round.

—Letter to Hamish Hamilton—December 4, 1949

Being, like all those who have worked in Hollywood, somewhat of a connoisseur of the damp fart.

—Letter to Dale Warren, October 2, 1946

You can live a long time in Hollywood and never see the part they use in pictures.

—*The Little Sister*

The motion picture is a great industry, as well as a defeated art.

—"Writers in Hollywood," *Atlantic Monthly*—November 1945

. . . the only art at which we of this generation have any possible chance to greatly excel.

—"Oscar Night in Hollywood," *Atlantic Monthly*—1946

I suppose in some ways I was a bit of a stinker in Hollywood. I kept the money. No swimming pool, no stone marten coats for a floosie in an apartment, no charge account at Romanoff's, no parties, no ranch with riding horses, none of the trimmings at all. As a result of which I have fewer friends but a lot more money.

—Letter to Dale Warren—September 15, 1949

Real cities have something else, some individual bony structure under the muck. Los Angeles has Hollywood—and hates it. It ought to consider itself damn lucky. Without Hollywood it would be a mail-order city. Everything in the catalogue you could get better somewhere else.

—*The Little Sister*

For his first paid writing Chandler received precisely one cent per word from *Black Mask*. For his first long-term Hollywood screenwriting assignment he did rather better—$1,750 a week at Paramount. It was 1944 and he was fifty-six years old with four novels behind him that had now built a solid reputation.

Between 1944 and 1951 he worked on seven screenplays for Paramount, Warner Bros., MGM and Universal, but it was at Paramount that he had his most satisfactory relationship. In 1945 he was given a three-year contract calling for two scripts a year. He would receive $50,000 a year, whether or not he actually delivered the scripts. His agent, "Swanie" Swanson, also managed over the years to sell six of Chandler's novels to be made into movies. All in all, Hollywood was good to Raymond Chandler—at least financially.

Chandler took it all—as he took most things—with the proverbial pinch of salt or dash of bitters . . .

> If my books had been any worse, I should not have been invited to Hollywood, and if they had been any better, I should not have come.
>
> —Letter to Charles Morton—December 12, 1945

In fact, the Paramount contract was the result of an earlier one-off job. In 1943 he had been hired to collaborate with writer/director Billy Wilder on the screenplay of *Double Indemnity*—an ironic piece of casting in the light of his views on its author, James M. Cain. Neither Wilder nor Chandler was an easy man to work with, and the neophyte Chandler found the chore "an agonizing experience and has probably shortened my life." However, he admitted, "I learned from it as much about screen writing as I am capable of learning, which is not very much." He also earned $750 a week for thirteen weeks.

Initially Wilder found his new partner "peculiar, a sort of rather acid man" but later gave him credit for being "one of the greatest creative minds I've ever encountered." "We would start scene by scene

The Bronson Gate at Paramount—the most famous gate in Hollywood. Originally named United Studios when it was built in 1917, the studio was taken over in 1926 by Famous Players–Lasky and renamed Paramount. It's now the only major studio operating in Hollywood. Chandler worked here on Double Indemnity *and* The Blue Dahlia *between 1943 and 1946.* Photofest

and we started with the dialogue . . . And he was very good at that, just very, very good."

"He was a dilettante. He did not like the structure of a screenplay, wasn't used to it. He was a mess but he could write a beautiful sentence. 'There is nothing as empty as an empty swimming pool.' That is a great line" (*Conversations with Wilder*—1999).

What had attracted Wilder in the first place was reading in *The High Window* the phrase "He had hair growing out of his ear long enough to catch a moth." "How often do you read a description of a character [like that]?" Wilder asked. "Not many people write like that." Nonetheless, he added in counterbalance, Chandler gave him "more trouble than any other writer I ever worked with" and he had no intention of working with him again.

Chandler chats with Fred MacMurray on the set of Double Indemnity.

1943. Chandler and Billy Wilder at Paramount during the writing of Double Indemnity.
Bodleian Library, Oxford

Chandler's critical assessment of the screenwriting trade in his 1945 *Atlantic Monthly* article particularly incensed him—

"What Hollywood did to Raymond Chandler. What did Raymond Chandler do to Hollywood? It reminds me of a curtain line in *Shanghai Gesture* [Josef von Sternberg's 1941 movie] where Mother Goddam finds out one of the whores in the brothel is her own daughter. A friend says, 'God will forgive you.' And Mother Goddam says, 'But will *I* forgive God?' That's how I feel about sons of bitches like Chandler. Will Hollywood forgive Raymond Chandler?" (*Billy Wilder in Hollywood*—2004)

Chandler was in Wilder's terms "a dilettante . . . I would take what he wrote, and structure it, and we would work on it . . . there was a lot of Hitler in Chandler" (*Conversations with Wilder*).

The script has some typical Chandler exchanges. Insurance salesman Walter Neff is attracted to Mrs. Dietrichson on his initial visit to her house. She tells him to come back tomorrow when her husband is home . . .

"I wonder if I know what you mean." "I wonder if you wonder." Phyllis Dietrichson *(Barbara Stanwyck) and Walter Neff (Fred MacMurray) start their deadly flirtation in* Double Indemnity *(1944).* Photofest

NEFF: Will you be here too?
DIETRICHSON: I guess so. I usually am.
NEFF: Same chair, same perfume, same anklet?
DIETRICHSON: I wonder if I know what you mean?
NEFF: I wonder if you wonder.

Since he had been given the assignment because the book's author was otherwise engaged (on another movie), Chandler couldn't resist changing Cain's original dialogue:

I don't think any of the changes made were in conflict with your basic conception. In fact, you would have had to make them yourself. I do not doubt that some of them might have been made better, but they had to be made.

A curious matter I'd like to call to your attention . . . is your dialogue. Nothing could be more easy and natural and to the point on paper, and yet it doesn't quite play. We tried it out by having a couple of actors do a scene right out of the book. It had a sort of remote effect that I was at a loss to understand. It came to me then that the effect of your written dialogue is only partly sound and sense. The rest of the effect is the appearance on the page. These unevenly shaped hunks of quick-moving speech hit the eye with a sort of explosive effect. You read the stuff in batches, not in individual speech and counterspeech. On the screen this is all lost and the essential mildness of the phrasing shows up as lacking in sharpness. They tell me that is the difference between photographic dialogue and written dialogue. For the screen everything has to be sharpened and pointed and wherever possible elided. But of course you know far more about it than I do.

—Letter to James M. Cain—March 20, 1944

So why, one wonders, was he telling him?

Even after he had been given parole from Hollywood, he would remain ambivalent about his own abilities in writing for the movies.

6520 Havenhurst Dr.
Hollywood 46
March 20th, 1944

Dear Jim:

It was very kind of you to send me an inscribed copy of your book and I'm very grateful to you. We have been down in the desert for a month, with poor luck inasmuch. I don't offer that as an excuse for not writing before, the fact being that I was so completely pooped after nine months at Paramount that I couldn't even make myself write a letter. Just sat and stared morosely out of the window at the sand dunes.

Very glad to hear Warners bought Mildred Pierce. It seems I may have had a chance to work on it for them, but Paramount was not too enthusiastic about loaning me. Everybody who has seen Double Indemnity likes it (everybody that has talked to me, at least). They feeling is that it is a pretty fine picture and for once an emotionally integrated story has got on the screen in the mood in which it was written. I don't think any of the changes we made were in conflict with your basic conception. In fact, you would have had to make them yourself. I do not doubt that some of them might have been made better, but they had to be made. The emotional integration is due to the fact that the three guys who worked on the job did not at any time disagree about what they wanted to achieve, but only on how to achieve it.

A curious matter I'd like to call to your attention—although you have probably been all through it with yourself—is your dialogue. Nothing could be more natural and easy and to the point on paper,

Letter from Chandler to James M. Cain after the successful release of Double Indemnity.
Courtesy Craig Temmey

2.

and yet it doesn't quite play. We tried it out by having a couple of actors do a scene right out of the book. It had a sort of remote effect that I was at a loss to understand. It came to me then that the effect of your written dialogue is only partly sound and sense. The rest of the effect is the appearance on the page. These unevenly shaped hunks of quick-moving speech hit the eye with a sort of explosive effect. You read the stuff in batches, not in individual speech and counterspeech. On the screen this is all lost, and the essential mildness of the phrasing shows up as lacking in sharpness. They tell me that is the difference between photographable dialogue and written dialogue. For the screen everything has to be sharpened and pointed and wherever possible elided. But of course you know far more about that than I do.

I hope you get as good a script of Mildred Pierce. You don't need one quite so sharp. Are you working on it yourself?

All the best.

Ray Chandler

March 25, 1944

Mr. Raymond Chandler
1040 Havenhurst Drive
Hollywood 46, California

Dear Raymond:

Thanks for your note. The observation
that dialogue in my novels is calculated for
the eye rather than the ear is quite correct.
I use a completely different system in picture
work when I dictate for the ear and pay almost
no attention to how it appears to the eye. I
have often been secretly amused at picture
producers who tell me, "And don't forget to
give me plenty of that fast Cain dialogue."
The truth is the fast Cain dialogue wouldn't
play at all, but I think it advisable not to
tell them so.

Your description of the vague, cloudy
way the dialogue sounded when you had it
tried out with actors is wholly interesting,
for in "Double Indemnity" I was trying to
capture some of those bellowing unrealities
that you get in a fever dream, and if the
dialogue sounded as you say it did, quite
possibly I succeeded. It was pleasant to
hear from you, and on seeing the picture
a second time the other night I can only
repeat what I said before that it is a
beautiful job of writing and reflects the
greatest of credit on you. Please remember
me to your wife.

With best regards,

JRC/l

Cain's reply . . .

Walter Neff (Fred MacMurray) in the death chamber, watched by Edward G.
Robinson. An ending that Wilder shot, then discarded. Photofest

In 1951 he writes to Dale Warren (November 7), "It's not my cup of
tea, but it could have been if I'd started it twenty years earlier."

But in 1944 he is still the kid taking the clock apart and peering
at the works:

> Like every writer, or almost every writer who goes to Hollywood,
> I was convinced in the beginning that there must be some discov-
> erable method of working in pictures which would not be com-
> pletely stultifying to whatever creative talent one might happen
> to possess. But like others before me I discovered that this was a
> dream. It's nobody's fault; it's part of the structure of the industry.
> Too many people have too much to say about a writer's work. It
> ceases to be his own. And after a while he ceases to care about
> it. He has brief enthusiasms, but they are destroyed before they
> can flower. People who can't write tell him how to write . . . The
> wise screen writer is he who wears his second-best suit, artistically
> speaking, and doesn't take things too much to heart. He should

have a touch of cynicism, but only a touch. The complete cynic is as useless to Hollywood as he is to himself. He should do the best he can without straining at it. He should be scrupulously honest about his work, but he should not expect scrupulous honesty in return. He won't get it. And when he has had enough, he should say goodbye with a smile, because for all he knows he may want to go back.

These were recollections in tranquility told to Hamish Hamilton in 1950. Along the way he had not always felt so tolerant . . .

Long before the invitation came, he would write to George Harmon Coxe (April 9, 1939):

Personally I think Hollywood is poison to any writer, the graveyard to talent. I have always thought so. But perhaps I have lived too close to it . . . New writers do not appear to replace the ones who go to Hollywood and either stay there or learn how not to write there and never get over it.

Hammett, for instance,

was one of the many guys who couldn't take Hollywood without trying to push God out of the high seat.

Having tried it for himself . . .

Better men than I have gone to grease in Hollywood.

Three years in Hollywood leaves its mark. My kind of writing takes a certain quality of high spirits and impudence. I'm a tired character, a battered pulp writer, an out of work hack.
                    —Letter to Hamish Hamilton—October 6, 1946

The screenplay as it exists is the result of a bitter and prolonged struggle between the writer (or writers) and the people whose aim it is to exploit his talent without giving it the freedom to be a talent.
                    —Letter to Charles Morton—December 18, 1944

The writing of a screenplay is drudgery, partly because it is a difficult form and intrinsically unsatisfying, and partly because ninety-nine people know more about how it should be done than the one who does it . . . no screenwriter knows what he is doing. It takes somebody who is not a screenwriter to tell him what he is doing.

To write effectively for the screen you have to understand the grim obstacles and the mechanical processes which intervene between the script and the final negative . . . You go in with dreams, and you come out with the Parent-Teachers' Association.

"Good original screenplays are almost as rare in Hollywood as virgins."

—Letter to Erle Stanley Gardner—January 29, 1946

When writing the screenplay of *Playback*—for which he was paid $100,000 and which was never produced—and which he then turned into the novel of the same name—

Anyone would think I was building a pyramid . . . Now I have to polish it, as they say. Which means leave out half and make what is left hammier. This is a very delicate art and about as fascinating as scraping teeth.

—To Hamish Hamilton—October 27, 1947

Certainly it was hard work, but it was the *only* work.

The basic art of motion pictures is the screenplay; it is fundamental, without it there is nothing.

But even with it, the problems remained epic . . .

I am not interested in why the Hollywood system exists . . . I am interested only in the fact that as a result of it there is no such thing as an art of the screenplay, and there never will be as long as the system lasts, for it is the essence of this system that it seeks to exploit a talent without permitting it the right to be a talent. It cannot be done, you can only destroy the talent, which is exactly what happens—when there is any talent to destroy . . .

—"Writers in Hollywood"

The overall picture, as the boys say, is of a degraded community whose idealism even is largely fake.

—Letter to Alfred Knopf—January 12, 1946

Why *was* there no "art of the screenplay"?

The reason is at least partly that there exists no available body of technical theory and practice by which it can be learned. There is no available library of screenplay literature, because the screenplays belong to the studios, and they will only show them within their guarded walls . . . In fact, no part of the vast body of technical knowledge which Hollywood contains is systematically and as a matter of course made available to the new writer in a studio. They tell him to look at pictures—which is to learn architecture by staring at a house.

—"Writers in Hollywood"—1945

Most writers in Hollywood are employees . . . As an individual I refuse to be an employee, but of course I am only an individual.

—"Critical Notes"—1947

As an individual he was appalled by the back-of-the-hand treatment most writers received when it came to the finished film. His or her name would be "the last and least to be mentioned" in any promotional material . . .

This neglect is of no consequence to me personally; to any writer of books a Hollywood by-line is trivial.

—"Writers in Hollywood"

"Big production, no story, as they say around the movie lots."

—*The Long Goodbye*

I wish I could write the Hollywood novel that has never been written, but it takes a more photographic memory than I have. The whole scene is too complex . . .

—Letter to Edward Weeks—February 27, 1957

I wish to God Hollywood would stop trying to be significant, because when art is significant, it is always a by-product and more or less unintentional on the part of the creator.

Chandler was clear about what the screenwriter's job involved: "The content of a motion picture is character and emotion and situation, and the combination of these things into drama."

. . . The best scenes I ever wrote were practically monosyllabic. And the best short scene I ever wrote, by my own judgment, was one in which a girl said "uh huh" three times with three different intonations, and that's all there was to it . . . The hell of good film writing is that the most important part is what is left out. It's left out because the camera and the actors can do it better and quicker, above all quicker. But it had to be there in the beginning.

—Letter to Dale Warren—November 7, 1951

Overall, he had little time for his fellow scribes . . .

Hollywood is easy to hate, easy to sneer at, easy to lampoon. Some of the lampooning has been done by people who have never walked through a studio gate, some of the best sneering by ego-centric geniuses who departed huffily—not forgetting to collect their last pay check—leaving nothing behind them but the exqui-site aroma of their personalities and a botched job for the tired hacks to clear up.

—"Writers in Hollywood"—1945

Writers as a class I have found to be over-sensitive and spiritually undernourished. They have the egotism of actors and rarely the good looks or charm . . . That's one thing I like about Holly-wood. The writer is there revealed in his ultimate corruption. He asks no praise, because the praise comes to him in the form of a salary check. In Hollywood, the average writer is not young, not brave, and a bit over-dressed.

He did, however, have one thing to commend him to Chandler:

But he is darn good company.
—Letter to Lenore Offord—December 6, 1948

As for actors . . .

"There was a time when actors went in at the back door. Most of them still should."
—Mavis Weld, movie star, in *The Little Sister*

"He's the fellow for whom they coined the phrase, 'as ignorant as an actor.' "
—*The High Window*

. . . and producers . . .

"Some are able and humane men and some are low grade indi-viduals with the morals of a goat, the artistic integrity of a slot machine, and the manners of a floorwalker with delusions of grandeur."
—"Writers in Hollywood"

Some Hollywood big shot . . . some wizard of the slobbery kiss, and the pornographic dissolve.
—*The Little Sister*

In *The Little Sister* the producer Jules Oppenheimer gives Marlowe a lesson on the basics of the film industry. It starts with owning fifteen hundred theaters (which he just happens to do):

"The motion picture business is the only business in the world in which you can make all the mistakes in the world and still make money . . . You have to have the fifteen hundred theaters."

"That makes it a little harder to get a start," I said.

"When in doubt, have two guys come through the door with guns in their fists."

"The really good mystery picture has not yet been made, unless by Hitchcock, and that is a rather different kind of picture. *The Maltese Falcon* came closest."

The reason is that the detective in the picture has to fall for some girl, whereas the real distinction of the detective's personality is that, as a detective, he falls for nobody. He is the avenging justice, the bringer of order out of chaos, and to make his doing this part of a trite boy-meets-girl story is to make it silly. But in Hollywood you cannot make a picture which is not essentially a love story, that is to say, a story in which sex is paramount.

—Letter to Jean Bethel—April 20, 1947

But for all the frustration he had experienced by that time he could still admit in 1948 that the movies represented "the only original art the modern world has conceived" (*Atlantic Monthly*—March) and that a bad film does not mean that the medium itself is necessarily bad. "If Hollywood makes money out of poor pictures, it could make more money out of good ones."

Some of the difficulty was symbolically expressed by Leo, one of the characters in the film: "Just don't get too complicated, Eddie. When a guy gets complicated, he's unhappy. And when he's unhappy—his luck runs out."

Houseman was contracted to produce a starring vehicle for Alan Ladd, Paramount's current hot property. The only problem was that the war was still on and Ladd had a firm call-up date from the army—a booking that overrode all other commitments. The film could not afford to go over its rather tight shooting schedule.

Houseman called Chandler . . .

Veronica Lake as Joyce Harwood in The Blue Dahlia. *"Every guy's seen you before—somewhere. The trick is to find you."* Photofest

Lake had been teamed with Ladd in the earlier The Glass Key *and* This Gun for Hire *(both 1942). She was one of the few current leading ladies petite enough to play opposite the diminutive Ladd.*

In less than two weeks I wrote an original story of 90 pages. All dictated and never looked at until finished. It was an experiment and for a guy subject from early childhood to plot-constipation, it was rather a revelation. Some of the stuff is good, some very much not.

—Letter to Charles Morton—January 15, 1945

He felt he had developed a useful *modus operandi*:

I don't see why the method could not be adopted to novel-writing, at least by me. Improvise the story as well as you can, in as much detail or as little as the mood seems to suggest, write dialogue or leave it out, but cover the movement, the characters, and bring the thing to life . . .

Possibly—I'm not sure—the rejuvenation of the motion picture, if and when it comes, will have to be through some such process of writing directly for the screen and almost under the camera . . . its true business is to photograph dramatic movement

John Houseman (1902–1988). Stage, film, radio and TV producer, best known for his collaboration with Orson Welles on The War of the Worlds. *Later he became an Oscar-winning actor. "We once wrote a picture called* The Blue Dahlia, *remember? It may not have been the best but at least we tried. And the circumstances were a bit difficult . . ."* Photofest

Chandler in 1945 working on The Blue Dahlia, *his only original screenplay.* Photofest

from the simplest possible angles—those of the two eyes . . . Moving the camera has become a substitute for moving the action, and this is recession.

—Letters to Charles W. Morton—January/March 1945

However, the pressures of time and the speed of director George Marshall's shooting soon produced a crisis. Marshall was shooting the pages of the script faster than Chandler was writing them. "Any day now an expensive crew would be standing around looking at each other with the taxi meter running."

Houseman recalled the way the problem was solved—a story in its way as dramatic as anything in the film. Chandler came to him and said that the only way he could complete the task in time was to write while he was drunk. Even then (1945) he had a serious drinking problem, and he knew he was endangering his health with what he was proposing. Nonetheless, it was a straw Houseman reluctantly snatched at and for the next several weeks there was round-the-clock limo transportation standing by, six secretaries working in shifts to take Chandler's dictation, and a doctor on call to give him glucose injections in lieu of solid food.

Amazingly, it worked. The film was finished with six days to spare. Alan Ladd went off to the army. And Paramount Studios not only didn't go bankrupt—which had been a genuine risk—but made $2,750,000, a lot of money in those days. In due course, Chandler was nominated for his second Academy Award. Again he did not win, and one might speculate that his outspoken criticism of Hollywood, its manners and mores, might have been a contributing factor.

Despite his success, Chandler continued to find fault with the studio process.

> It is ludicrous to suggest that any writer in Hollywood, however obstreperous, has a "free hand" with a script; he may have a free hand with the first draft but after that they start moving in on him. Also what happens on the set is beyond the writer's control. In this case I threatened to walk off the picture, not yet finished, unless they stopped the director putting in fresh dialogue out of his own head . . .
> —Letter to James Sandoe—October 2, 1947

But his concerns about studio practice were dwarfed by the diktat of an even mightier power—the U.S. Navy. Well into the shooting, they questioned Chandler's intended solution to the story . . .

> What the Navy Department did to the story was a little thing like making me change the murderer and hence make a routine whodunit out of a fairly original idea. What I wrote was the story of a man who killed (executed would be a better word) his pal's wife under the stress of a great and legitimate anger, then blanked out and forgot all about it; then with perfect honesty did his best to help the pal get out of a jam, then found himself in a set of circumstances which brought about partial recall. The poor guy

remembered enough to make it clear who the murderer was to others but never realized it himself. He just did and said things he couldn't have done or said unless he was the killer; but he never knew he did them or said them and never interpreted them.

—Letter to James Sandoe—June 17, 1946

The Navy, however, had a war it was still fighting, and it was not about to have an injured service man depicted as a killer, however well-intentioned. Chandler had no option but to twist the remaining plot to make the janitor the murderer—a version of the old cliché . . . "The butler did it."

Apart from that, Chandler was wrong to be overly critical of *The Blue Dahlia*. Nonetheless, he was. He was particularly disturbed by the female lead, Veronica Lake ("Miss Moronica Lake"):

The only times she's good is when she keeps her mouth shut and looks mysterious. The moment she tries to behave as if she had a brain she falls flat on her face. The scenes we had to cut out because she loused them up! And there are three godawful close shots of her looking perturbed that make me want to throw my lunch over the fence.

—Letter to James Sandoe—May 20, 1946

Ladd and Lake may not have had the chemistry Bogart and Bacall would have in *The Big Sleep* that same year, but they did have some typical Chandler dialogue . . .

JOYCE: I suppose you've seen me before?
JOHNNY: Have I?
JOYCE: Probably. I used to work in a dance hall down on Main Street.
JOHNNY: Yes, I've seen you before alright. But not in any dance hall and not in any Main Street.
JOYCE: Where, then?
JOHNNY: Every guy's seen you before—somewhere. The trick is to find you. And when he does, it's usually too late.

Later, in whimsical mood, Chandler would envision . . .

a remake of *King of Kings* with Alan Ladd as Christ, Cecil B. deMille as God and Betty Hutton as the Virgin Mary. But I bet Bill Bendix steals the picture as Mary Magdalene.
                    —Letter to H. N. Swanson—October 15, 1948

Part of the problem, it must be said, was Chandler's own attitude toward those he worked with . . .

The only employer I ever had that I got along with was Paramount Studios and there as a matter of course one began each day by telling everybody to go to hell. They even seemed to like that.

The picture business can be a little trying at times, but I don't suppose working at General Motors is all sheer delight.

Los Angeles . . . a city where pretty faces are as common as runs in dollar stockings.

It was the artificiality that particularly grated on his cynical psyche:

Malibu. More movie stars. More pink and blue bathtubs. More tufted beds. More Chanel No. 5. More Lincoln Continentals and Cadillacs. More wind-blown hair and sunglasses and pseudo-refined voices and waterfront morals.
                    —*The Little Sister*

The bar [*of the mythical Ritz-Beverly Hotel*] was pretty empty. Three booths down a couple of sharpies were selling each other pieces of Twentieth Century–Fox, using double-arm gestures instead of money. They had a telephone on the table between them and every two or three minutes they would play the match game to see who called Zanuck with a hot idea. They were young, dark, eager and full of vitality. They put as much muscular activity into a telephone conversation as I would put into carrying a fat man up four flights of stairs.

—*The Long Goodbye*

Today those dark, eager young men would be competing to see who had the smallest cell phone.

"What I like about this place is everything runs true to type. The cop on the gate, the shine on the door, the cigarette and check girls, the fat greasy Jew with the tall stately bored showgirl, the well-dressed, drunk and horribly rude director cursing the barman, the silent guy with the gun, the night club owner with the soft gray hair and the B-picture mannerisms, and now you—the dark torcher with the negligent sneer, the husky voice, the hard-boiled vocabulary."

"And what about the wise-cracking snooper with the last year's gags and the come-hither smile?"

—Marlowe and Linda Conquest in *The High Window*

Morny's nightclub was like a high-budget musical:

a lot of light and glitter, a lot of scenery, a lot of clothes, a lot of sound, an all-star cast, and a plot with all the originality and drive of a split fingernail.

—*The High Window*

In Hollywood everybody and everything—whether it knows it or not—acts like it was in a Hollywood movie. In *The Big Sleep*, small-time gangster Joe Brody's voice was

the elaborately casual voice of the tough guy in pictures. Pictures have made them all like that.

Now, Voyager (1942) was famous for Paul Henreid's trick of lighting two cigarettes and passing one to Bette Davis:

"May I have a cigarette?"

"The old cigarette stall," I said. I got a couple out and put them in my mouth and lit them. I leaned across and tucked one between her ruby lips.

"Nothing's cornier than that," she said. "Except maybe butterfly kisses."

"Sex is a wonderful thing," I said. "When you don't want to answer questions."

—*The Little Sister*

He glanced at his fingernails one by one, holding them up against the light and studying them with care, as Hollywood has taught it should be done.

—*The Big Sleep*

The only thing the matter with him for a movie newshawk was that he wasn't drunk.

—"Bay City Blues"

"Why do we need the moon when we have the stars?" But first let's have a cigarette . . . Paul Henreid lights up Bette Davis in Warner Bros.' 1942 Now, Voyager. Photofest

She looked smart, but not Hollywood-smart.

> —"Mandarin's Jade"

The balcony was high and the scene down below had a patterned look, like an overhead camera shot.

> —"Nevada Gas"

A dark-haired waiter who looked like a road company Herbert Marshall.

> —*Playback*

"Early Lillian Gish," Morny said. "Very early Lillian Gish . . . Don't feed me the ham. I've been in pictures. I'm a connoisseur of ham."

> —*The High Window*

A voice that sounded like Orson Welles with his mouth full of crackers.

> —*The Little Sister*

I knew he would call right back. They always do when they think they're tough. They haven't used their exit line.

> —*The Little Sister*

He brought the gun up hard and straight, like the wicked fore-man of the Lazy Q.

> —*The Little Sister*

I took hold of the outstretched arm and spun him around. "What's the matter, Jack? Don't they make the aisles wide enough for your personality?"

He shook his arm loose and got tough. "Don't get fancy, buster. I might loosen your jaw for you."

"Ha, ha," I said. "You might play center field for the Yankees and hit a home run with a breadstick."

He doubled a meaty fist.

"Darling, think of your manicure," I told him.

He controlled his emotions. "Nuts to you, wise guy," he sneered. "Some other time, when I have less on my mind."

"Could there be less?"

"G'wan, beat it," he snarled. "One more crack and you'll need new bridgework."

I grinned at him. "Call me up, Jack. But with better dialogue."

His expression changed. He laughed. "You in pictures, chum?"

"Only the kind they pin up in the post office."

"See you in the mug book," he said, and walked away still grinning.

—*The Long Goodbye*

"Hollywood Boulevard, my foot. A lot of bit players out of work and fish-faced blondes trying to shake a hangover out of their teeth."

—"Bay City Blues"

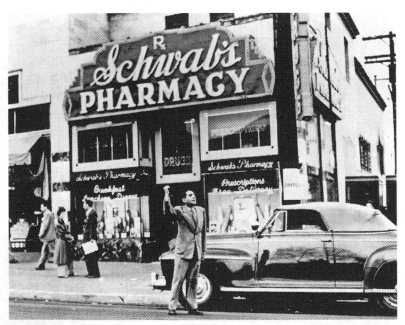

Schwab's Pharmacy on Sunset and Crescent Heights. Despite the publicity, Lana Turner was not discovered there on a bar stool, but the landmark drugstore-cum-boutique was much frequented by the Hollywood crowd. Photofest

You have to have your teeth clamped around Hollywood to keep from chewing on stray blondes.

—*The Big Sleep*

The kid said: "I don't like drunks in the first place and in the second place I don't like them getting drunk here, and in the third place I don't like them in the first place."

"Warner Brothers could use that," I said.

"They did."

—"Red Wind"

The star was a bad-tempered brunette with contemptuous eyes and a couple of bad close-ups that showed her pushing forty-five backwards almost hard enough to break a wrist.

—*The Little Sister*

Wonderful what Hollywood will do to a nobody. It will make a radiant glamour queen out of a drab little wench who ought to be ironing a truck driver's shirts, a he-man hero with shining eyes and brilliant smile reeking of sexual charm out of some overgrown kid who was meant to go to work with a lunchbox. Out of a Texas car hop with the literacy of a character in a comic strip it will make an international courtesan, married six times to six millionaires and so blasé and decadent at the end of it that her idea of a thrill is to seduce a furniture mover in a sweaty undershirt.

—*The Little Sister*

"Screen stars, phooey. The veterans of a thousand beds."

—Marlowe in *The Little Sister*

In Hollywood anything can happen, anything at all.

—*The Long Goodbye*

One thing that was happening while Chandler was occupied with *The Blue Dahlia* was the film version of *The Big Sleep*, directed by

Dick Powell plays Marlowe opposite Claire Trevor in Murder, My Sweet, *released abroad as* Farewell, My Lovely *(1944).*

Howard Hawks for Warner Bros. and starring Humphrey Bogart and Lauren Bacall.

It was not the first film version of a Chandler novel—simply the best.

Farewell, My Lovely and *The High Window* had already been sold to RKO and 20th Century Fox respectively, only to be turned into standard episodes of ongoing B-picture series.

Farewell, My Lovely became the 1942 *The Falcon Takes Over,* a starring vehicle for George Sanders and itself a rip-off of *The Saint* series; while *The High Window* became the 1942 *Time to Kill* with Lloyd Nolan as the series character Michael Shayne.

But with the success of *Double Indemnity* Raymond Chandler was suddenly a hot property, and some rapid studio rethinking went on. RKO still had the rights to *Farewell, My Lovely* and quickly remade it, giving Dick Powell—a fading star of 1930s Warner musicals—his first dramatic role and effectively relaunching his career. In their wisdom they decided the title would not do—it might suggest another Powell musical—so it was retitled (in the U.S., at least) *Murder, My Sweet* and released in 1944.

It was a much better effort than the first one and remarkably faithful to the original novel, even though it suffered the by now expected slings and arrows of the Production Code. Some of the violence had to be toned down, but director Edward Dmytryk caught Marlowe's "voice" by the simple expedient of using a good deal of voice-over first-person narrative taken from the text . . .

> "OK, Marlowe," I said to myself. "You're a tough guy. You've been sapped twice, choked, beaten silly with a gun, shot in the arm until you're crazy as a couple of waltzing mice. Now let's see you do something really tough—like putting your pants on."

Chandler liked the film and Powell as Marlowe; although the actor would not have been his first choice, he would say later that Powell was the closest of the screen Marlowes to his original conception. He had originally seen Cary Grant in the role—just as Ian Fleming was to have Grant in mind for James Bond some years later.

Nevertheless, he was perfectly happy when Warner Bros. used their own contract star, Humphrey Bogart, for their version of *The Big Sleep*. Bogart was riding high after a succession of romantic tough guy roles—*High Sierra* (1941), *The Maltese Falcon* (1941), *To Have and Have Not* (1944)—and *The Big Sleep* reunited him with director Howard Hawks and costar Lauren Bacall, soon to be his wife.

Bogart—Chandler felt—was

> the genuine article . . . He can be tough without a gun . . . Bogart is superb as Bogart . . . Also he has a sense of humor that contains that grating undertone of contempt. Ladd is hard, bitter and occasionally charming, but he is after all a small boy's idea of a tough guy.

"When and if you see *The Big Sleep*," he wrote to Hamish Hamilton, "you will realize what can be done with this sort of story by a director with a gift of atmosphere and the requisite touch of hidden sadism."

Bogart was intrigued by Marlowe but had one question for Chandler. Why didn't Marlowe go overboard for the girl? Chandler had an answer for him:

> Marlowe would lose something by being promiscuous. I know he can't go on forever saying no the way he does—the guy's human—he'll have to break sometime but I've never wanted the sex bit to dominate either him or the story.

His contract with Paramount prohibited Chandler from being involved in the film but he and Hawks got to know each other and met regularly. There is a story about the shoot, which many consider apochryphal but which is almost certainly true.

Hawks and his scriptwriters—William Faulkner, Jules Furthman and Leigh Brackett—were getting confused by the book's plot, even though they were managing to incorporate a substantial amount of the book into their screenplay. One day Hawks cabled Chandler to ask who, in fact, had killed the Sternwoods' chauffeur. Chandler cabled back: "NO IDEA." It was an answer that tied in with his basic

Howard Hawks (1896–1977), director of The Big Sleep. Photofest

The Lady in the Lake *(1946). Director and star Robert Montgomery experimented with the I-am-a-camera technique. Audiences saw Montgomery's face only when he looked in a mirror. Costar Audrey Totter shows Marlowe the results of a run-in with some unfriendly individuals.*
Photofest

philosophy of the genre in which he worked. He was interested, he said, in "what happened, rather than whodunit."

Hawks came up with a nice in-joke during the film. In one scene Marlowe goes to a public library. While he is there a sweet young librarian suggests he read an excellent new thriller that has just come in . . . "Raymond Chandler's latest. What a picture *that'll* make."

The Big Sleep was a huge box office success and Warner Bros. made a nice profit on their $10,000 investment. Something of Marlowe rubbed off on Bogart for the rest of his career, and at least one of Chandler's handful of novels received a definitive film treatment.

Chandler himself moved from *The Blue Dahlia* to an assignment for MGM. He was to work on the film version of *Lady in the Lake*.

It was not a happy experience. MGM was more bureaucratically run than Paramount and it didn't take as kindly to being told to go to hell. The pressures to conform were so irksome and the task of adaptation so tedious—he even resorted to putting in scenes that weren't in the book—that after three months' desultory work he gave up and walked out. It was "just turning over dry bones."

Director and star Robert Montgomery decided to shoot the film with an I-am-a-camera technique, so that the viewer would see only what Marlowe saw. In more experienced directorial hands it might have worked passably well, but with Montgomery it merely seemed an affectation. To Chandler it was "old stuff." "Let's make the camera a character; it's been said at every lunch table in Hollywood one time or another." He refused to accept screen credit.

Despite his reputation for being "difficult"—or perhaps because of it—the Hollywood studios continued to beat a path to his door. Paramount had to write off another large sum as yet another project failed to hold his attention. Sam Goldwyn tried to persuade him to return to MGM, and that encounter at least amused him. ("I suppose everyone ought to meet Samuel Goldwyn this side of Paradise.")

His most effective film writing at this stage—late 1945—was *about* film writing.

> What Hollywood seems to want is a writer who is ready to commit suicide in every story conference. What it actually gets is the fellow who screams like a stallion in heat and then cuts his throat with a banana. The scream demonstrates the artistic purity of his soul and he can eat the banana while somebody is answering a telephone call about some other picture . . .
> —"Hollywood and the Screen Writer"

In 1946 Chandler left Hollywood. He and Cissy moved back to La Jolla. It was time to get back to his novels. He wrote to Alfred Knopf (January 12, 1946):

> [Hollywood is] a sweet subject for a novel—probably the greatest still untouched . . .
> It is like one of those South American palace revolutions conducted by officers in comic opera uniforms—only when the

thing is over the ragged men lie in rows against the wall, and you suddenly know that this is not funny, this is the Roman Circus, and damn near the end of civilization.

"Money is no longer a compelling motive, unless I could make it by writing books. If I can't, I can always make it in the Hollywood slaughter house, ankle-deep in blood and screaming like a Saracen."

—Letter to John Hersey—March 29, 1948

It was to be *au revoir* and not goodbye, as things turned out. In 1950 he was offered $2,500 a week by Warner Bros. to adapt Patricia Highsmith's novel *Strangers on a Train* for Alfred Hitchcock to direct.

Why am I doing it? Partly because I thought I might like Hitch, which I do, and partly because one gets tired of saying no, and someday I might want to say yes and not get asked.

In theory it should have worked out well. Two expatriate "Englishmen" who had learned to deal with Americans; both masters of suspense. But therein lay the problem. Chandler found Hitchcock "as nice as can be to argue with" but he also found him intractable. A Hitchcock film would always be a "Hitchcock film."

One thing that amuses me about Hitchcock is the way he directs a film in his head before he knows what the story is. You find yourself trying to rationalize the shots he wants to make rather than the story. Every time you get set he jabs you off balance by wanting to do a love scene on top of the Jefferson Memorial or something like that.

—Letter to Hamish Hamilton—September 4, 1950

This time, before Chandler could walk, he was pushed. Hitchcock fired him. Two creative voices—particularly these two—were one too many. Chandler received $40,000 for his contribution and reluctantly accepted co-writing credit on the finished picture, which he described as "no guts, no characters, no plausability [*sic*], and no dialogue . . . but of course it's Hitchcock, and a Hitchcock film always does have something."

"I don't know why it's a success, perhaps because Hitchcock succeeded in removing almost every trace of my writing from it."

The screenplay he had turned in—he rationalized later—"had too much Chandler in it and not enough Hitchcock." It was rewritten by one Czenzi Ormonde.

But the experience clearly bothered him. In November he wrote to Finley McDermid:

Are you aware that this screenplay was written without one single consultation with Mr. Hitchcock after the writing of the screenplay began? Not even a telephone call. Not one word of criticism or appreciation. Silence. Blank silence then and since. You are

Two strangers—Farley Granger and Robert Walker—meet in Hitchcock's Strangers on a Train *(1951)*. Photofest

much too clever a man to believe that any writer will do his best in conditions like this. There are always things that need to be discussed. There are always places where a writer goes wrong, not being himself a master of the camera. There are always difficult little points which require the meeting of the minds, the accommodation of points of view. I had none of this. I find it rather strange. I find it rather ruthless. I find it almost incomparably rude.

Hitchcock—not surprisingly—remembered rather differently: "Our association didn't work out at all. We'd sit together and I would say—'Why not do it this way?'—and he'd answer—'Well, if you can puzzle it out, what do you need me for?' The work he did was no good and I ended up with Czenzi Ormonde, a woman writer who was one of Ben Hecht's assistants. When I completed the treatment, the head of Warner's tried to get someone to do the dialogue and very few writers would touch it" (*Hitchcock/Truffaut*).

But perhaps the real reason was that Chandler and Hitchcock had a fundamental difference of approach to this kind of material.

Hitchcock was the acknowledged master of "suspense" but Chandler felt that "suspense as an absolute quality has never seemed to me to be very important. At best it is a secondary growth, and at worst an attempt to make something out of nothing."

The film opens at the entrance of Union Station, Washington, D.C., with the usual bustle of a major terminal.

A taxi draws up. We see a porter being handed some luggage—among it several tennis rackets. The passenger gets out but we only see his shoes—dark brogues. We follow him as he begins to walk into the station.

A limousine now draws up and the pattern is repeated. This time the luggage is more impressive and the shoes a rather sporty black and white. They also walk into the station and we follow.

On the train they arrive more or less simultaneously in the parlor car and their owners take their seats. As they do, one of the sports shoes accidentally brushes against a brogue. As the owner of the sports shoe apologizes, the camera moves up to show the two owners of the shoes.

The sports shoes belong to Bruno Anthony, a young man in his mid-twenties who now recognizes his traveling companion as Guy Haines, a well-known tennis player.

Guy is a private sort of person with no wish to indulge in casual conversation with strangers.

Bruno, on the other hand, is the gregarious type. He tells Guy he knows him from the gossip columns: he's the secretary to a senator and rumor has it that he's to marry the senator's daughter. Guy points out that he is already married and tries to break off the conversation but Bruno will have none of it. He insists they have a drink.

He orders from the waiter, then takes out a cigarette, fumbles in his pocket but can't find a match.

Guy offers him his lighter, which, after lighting his cigarette, Bruno examines, seeing the distinctive symbol of a tennis club embossed on it next to the name GUY HAINES. He holds it rather longer than necessary but finally hands it back.

Worn down by Bruno's persistence, Guy admits that a divorce is indeed likely. He's on his way right now to discuss it with his wife before he goes on to a major tournament.

Bruno insists they have lunch in his compartment and we find them there after the meal. Bruno is by now a little worse for wear after a couple of drinks. He picks up Guy's lighter to light another cigarette and again takes his time returning it. It clearly fascinates him.

He has persuaded a reluctant Guy to talk about his failed marriage, and now Bruno begins to elaborate a little excitedly on what Guy has said. Clearly, to his mind, Miriam—Guy's wife—is a "tramp" . . . like all women. Someone should get rid of her.

This is too much for Guy and he makes as if to leave. Bruno quickly apologizes for being presumptuous to someone he barely knows. He then goes on to discuss his own family situation—a mother he adores and a father he hates—both to the point of obsession. A sudden inspiration strikes him. He and Guy have something in common after all. A problem person. Guy has his wife and he has his father. If only the problem people were to be murdered. Murder would be fun, don't you think, Guy?

What Guy thinks is that Bruno is drunk, and he can't wait to end the conversation politely.

Bruno is now on a dangerous high. He begins to elaborate. Why not swap murders? He'll kill Miriam and Guy can kill Bruno's father. Criss-cross. Two murders by strangers without a motive. Foolproof.

The train comes into a station and Guy leaves, relieved.

Bruno remains seated. He takes Guy's lighter out of his pocket and flicks it on and off thoughtfully.

End of scene.

Chandler and Hitchcock may not have seen eye to eye, but there was a moment when Chandler demonstrated the "Hitchcock Touch." Hitchcock was famous for liking to make a cameo appearance in his films as a "walk-on" extra. In *Double Indemnity* there's a scene between Neff and Keyes in Keyes's office. Neff leaves and turns left outside the door. As he begins to walk along the corridor, he passes a bench on which a man is sitting . . . Raymond Chandler.

> After approximately five years of working for Hollywood, I know that I wasn't meant to be a screenwriter . . . I am not trying to knock the art or profession of writing for the screen. This has to do with my private conception of what writing is, and what a writer is entitled to get out of his work, other than money. It has to do with magic and emotion and vision, with the free flow of images, thoughts and ideas, with discipline that comes from within and is not imposed from without . . . It has to do with that rare facility of expression which has nothing to do with conscious technique, since technique bears the same relation to it as a grammarian does to a poet . . . Without magic there is no art.
>
> I am not a sole screenplay writer, if by this crack is meant a creative artist who can all by himself produce a clean and wholesome shooting script which, as it stands, will satisfy all concerned

and fill them with jubilation. I am just not that good. At the risk of being thought a cad, may I ask who is?

Hollywood's failure to find an enlightened way of dealing with creative people is no longer merely a matter of bruised egos. It is a failure of a method of making pictures, and the results of this failure are showing up at the box office.

It's a disgraceful thing that no reputable writer can work for Hollywood without its ending in cynicism and disgust.

I shall probably do others [screenplays], and if so I shall do them as well as I know how, but I shall keep my heart to myself.

—Letter to Hamish Hamilton—November 10, 1950

He did not.

I think today there are much better film writers than I could ever be, because I never quite saw things in the terms of the camera, but always as dramatic scenes between people.

—Letter to Helga Greene—April 30, 1957

And finally, "A Qualified Farewell" (early 1950s) . . .

I have a sense of exile from thought, a nostalgia of the quiet room and the balanced mind. I am a writer and there comes a time when that which I write has to belong to me, has to be written alone and in silence, with no one looking over my shoulder, no one telling me a better way to write it. It doesn't have to be great writing, it doesn't even have to be terribly good. It just has to be mine.

His considered verdict in Hollywood—"I personally had a lot of fun there."

2014 and something that would have raised a wry Chandler smile. He is given a star on the Hollywood Walk of Fame.

Seven

Dames ... the Little Sisters

Trouble dwelt in her eyes.

—"No Crime in the Mountains"

At the bottom of his heart every decent man feels that his approach to the woman he loves is an approach to a shrine.

—Raymond Chandler

She sighed. "All men are the same."

"So are all women—after the first nine."

—Mrs. Grayle and Marlowe in *Farewell, My Lovely*

"Dames lie about anything—just for practice," Nulty said grimly.

—*Farewell, My Lovely*

In his private life—apart from a few desperate and irrelevant forays—he appears to have loved only one woman, Cissy, and he was happily married to her for over thirty years. By the time he watched her die he was a hopeless alcoholic and a self-doomed man himself. The last few years were a sad personal coda, as he persuaded himself he had fallen in love with and was about to marry a whole string of women—several of whom, like Natasha Spender, were in no position to marry him, since they were married already.

As John Houseman acutely observed—since, as an ex–English

public schoolboy himself, he understood Chandler's conditioning and the value system he took to the grave—"In life he was too inhibited to be gay; too emotional to be witty . . . the system had left a sexually devastating mark on him."

Houseman's assessment would seem to explain the offhand way Chandler so often treats women in his fiction. They fascinate and frighten him at the same time. There is little love, and even that is dispassionately handled . . . a certain amount of wariness toward dominating women . . .

> One of the women had enough ice on her to cool the Mojave Desert and enough make-up to paint a steam yacht . . . The men with them looked gray and tired, probably from signing checks.
> *—Playback*

. . . and a strong element of male chauvinism that treats women as sex objects, which, to be fair, was by no means unusual for the period . . .

Veronica Lake. Chandler was less than impressed with the performance of "Miss Moronica Lake." "The only times she's good," he said, "is when she keeps her mouth shut and looks mysterious." Photofest

Lauren Bacall as Vivian Rutledge in The Big Sleep *(1946). Chandler wrote of the character, called Vivian Regan in the book: "Her eyes were pools of darkness, much emptier than darkness."*
Photofest

[The cigarette girl] wore an egret-plume in her hair, enough clothes to hide behind a tooth pick, one of her long beautiful naked legs was silver and one was gold. She had the utterly disdainful expression of a dame who makes her dates by long distance.

Women *per se* are not to be trusted. In four of the seven novels the murderer is a woman. In all but one of them she is beautiful . . .

In "Blackmailers Don't Shoot" Rhonda Farr has "the sort of skin an old rake dreams of."

In "Try the Girl" Beulah has "hair like a brush fire at night"—which makes her a twin sister to Dolores Chiozza in "The King in Yellow," whose hair was "the color of a brush fire seen through a cloud of dust."

Belle Marr in "Spanish Blood" goes one better. Her hair "seemed to gather all the light there was and make a soft halo around her coldly beautiful face."

Under the skin, though, they were all sisters to Harriet Huntress in "Trouble Is My Business"—

She didn't look hard, but she looked as if she had heard all the answers and remembered the ones she thought she might be able to use sometime.

—or the girl in the cigarette kiosk in *Playback*:

I wouldn't say she looked exactly wistful, but neither did she look as hard to get as a controlling interest in General Motors.

Chandler—or Chandler through Marlowe—invariably notices the lady's eyes. Usually he sees danger in them: "Her eyes held a warm bitterness like poisoned honey" (of Mrs. Prendergast in "Mandarin's Jade") . . . "The woman's seaweed-colored eyes" (of Mrs. Shamey in "Try the Girl") . . . The hatcheck girl at the Idle Valley Club "had eyes like strange sins" (*The High Window*) . . . "Her eyes were pools of darkness, much emptier than darkness" (of Vivian Regan in *The Big Sleep*).

Sometimes the eyes have a second line of defense—

The mascara was so thick on her eyelashes that they looked like miniature iron railings.
                    —Of Mrs. Morny in *The High Window*

—although in this case it was Marlowe who needed the protection!

Much less threatening was Carol Pride in "Mandarin's Jade," whose "eyes could be very blue if they tried."

Then there was the way the lady smiled . . .

Mrs. Pendergast gives John Dalmas "a smile I could feel in my hip pocket" . . . and later, . . . "She returned my smile with an angel on its back" ("Mandarin's Jade").

She smiled at me and her teeth were as thin and sharp as a pauper's Christmas.
                    —Of Helen Matson in "Bay City Blues"

A silvery ripple of laughter that held the unspoiled naturalness of a bubble dance.

> — Of Mrs. Morny in *The High Window*

Marlowe has been looking appreciatively at an attractive woman at poolside in *The Long Goodbye*. But then:

She opened a mouth like a fire-bucket and laughed. That terminated my interest in her. I couldn't hear the laugh but the hole in her face when she unzipped her teeth was all I needed.

Her mouth looked like the prelude to a scream.

> —Of Vivian Regan in *The Big Sleep*

She laughed. It was a silly pooped-out little laugh like a child trying to be supercilious at a playroom tea party.

> —Of Mavis Weld in *The Little Sister*

"Put some rouge on your cheeks . . . You look like the snow maiden after a hard night with the fishing fleet."

But perhaps the two most extended pieces of Marlowe misogyny are the descriptions of "Blonde Agnes" Lozelle, the assistant he meets in Geiger's bookstore in *The Big Sleep*—

Her smile was tentative but could be persuaded to be nice . . . [but when she realizes what Marlowe is up to, the smile] was now hanging by its teeth and eyebrows and wondering what it would hit when it dropped . . . she was as sore as an alderman with the mumps . . . her face fell apart like a bride's pie crust . . . the smile came back, with a couple of corners badly dented.

—and the girl in the cigarette kiosk in *The Little Sister* who gives Marlowe the full benefit of her *femme fatale* act:

A straw blonde with a long neck and tired eyes . . . She had a low lingering voice with a sort of moist caress in it like a damp bath towel . . . She did something slow and elegant to the back of her head, exhibiting what seemed like more than one handful of blood-red fingernails in the process . . .

A deeply unimpressed Marlowe departs . . .

[I] made off before she threw a half-nelson on me . . . She was staring after me with an expression she probably would have said was thoughtful.

Many of Chandler's women suffer from what we would now call low self-esteem:

"I'm a tramp. I've smothered in too many hall bedrooms, stripped in too many filthy dressing rooms, missed too many meals, told too many lies to be anything else."
>> —Jean Adrian in "Guns at Cyrano's"

"We're all bitches. Some smile more than others, that's all."
>> —Mavis Weld in *The Little Sister*

"A half smart guy," she said with a tired sniff. "That's all I ever draw. Never once a guy that's smart all the way around the course. Never once."
>> I grinned at her. "Did I hurt your head much?"
>> "You and every other man I ever met."
>> —Blonde Agnes in *The Big Sleep*

Fortunately for Chandler (and Marlowe), feminism hadn't found its voice at the time he was writing. If it had, he would certainly have come up with an evocative simile for it. As it was, male chauvinism tended to rule when it came to describing women . . .

She had a good figure, if you liked them four sizes bigger below the waist than above it.
>> —*Farewell, My Lovely*

Audrey Totter as Adrienne Fromsett in The Lady in the Lake.
"She had a figure and didn't act stingy with it." Photofest

She had a figure and didn't act stingy with it.

—*The Lady in the Lake*

I looked down at her legs. I could see them all right and the flag
that marked the goal line was no larger than it had to be.

—*The Little Sister*

Velma's photo in *Farewell, My Lovely* shows that she has "nice legs
and generous with 'em."

"I like a well-crowded stocking myself."

—"Bay City Blues"

But appearances could all too often be deceptive . . .

From thirty feet away she looked like a lot of class. From ten feet
away she looked like something made up to be seen from thirty
feet away.

—Of Mrs. Morny in *The High Window*

"I've seen hard women, but she's the bluing on armor plate."
                                    —Of Carol Donovan in "Goldfish"

I left her with her virtue intact, but it was quite a struggle. She nearly won.

The sad fact of life is that men and women don't understand each other—and never will . . .

"Is Morny dangerous to women?"
    "Don't be Victorian, old top. Women don't call it danger."
                                    —*The High Window*

One of those sidelong looks that women think men don't understand, the kind that feels like a dentist's drill.
                                    —"Mandarin's Jade"

Women have so few defenses, but they certainly perform wonders with those they have.
                                    —*Playback*

Despite all the above, "American girls are terrific"—as Chandler had Marlowe conclude in *The Long Goodbye*—as long as they *stayed* girls. But "American wives take in too damn much territory":

The air began to be spattered with darlings and crimson finger nails.
    The goddam women will start waving their hands and screwing up their faces and tinkling their goddam bracelets and making with the packaged charm which later on in the evening has a slight but unmistakable odor of sweat.
                                    —*The Long Goodbye*

All the well-to-do and almost well-to-do crowd accomplish in their lives is an over-decorated home—the house beautiful for gracious living—a wife who, if she is young, plays tennis at the Beach Club, lies on the beach until her visible skin looks like brown sandpaper and feels the same, I have no doubt, swills several cocktails before dinner (almost always in company with friends), several highballs after dinner and ends up either being pawed by some other girl's husband or shrieking with laughter at some joke which hardly merits more than a mild "huh." If she is verging on middle age she is very chic in a tasteless way, talks a great deal about how she is going to have the guest room done over by some jerk with long sideburns, has her husband so tamed that he is afraid to sit down in some of the chairs, and however tired he may be, he must shower and shave and put on his white dinner jacket (in summer) because Mr. and Mrs. Whoosis are coming over to play bridge, which he hates almost as much as he hates Mr. and Mrs. Whoosis.

—Letter to Michael Gilbert—September 6, 1956

Chandler's older women tend to be either vague . . .

One of those ageless women you see around municipal offices everywhere in the world. They were never young and will never be old. They have no beauty, no charm, no style. They don't have to please anybody. They are safe. They are civil without quite being polite and intelligent and knowledgeable without any real interest in anything. They are what human beings turn into when they trade life for existence and ambition for security.

—*The Little Sister*

. . . or venal—like Jessie Florian in *Farewell, My Lovely*—

Her bathrobe was just something around her body . . . she was as cute as a washtub.

or Mrs. Murdock in *The High Window,* who had

large moist eyes with the sympathetic expression of wet stones , as hard as the bricks in her front walk . . . "a grand old war horse," I said. "A heart of gold, and the gold's buried good and deep."

In the Chandler Gallery of Leading Ladies, one of those who smiled and smiled and turned out to be the ultimate villainess was Carmen Sternwood in *The Big Sleep*:

> She was twenty or so, small and delicately put together, but she looked durable . . . She walked as if she were floating . . . Her eyes were slate-gray, and had almost no expression when they looked at me. She came over near me and smiled with her mouth and she had little sharp predatory teeth, as white as fresh orange pith and as shiny as porcelain. They glistened between her thin too taut lips.

She comes on to Marlowe on sight.

> "You're cute," she giggled. "I'm cute, too."

When her father subsequently mentions his younger daughter, Marlowe replies:

> "I met her in the hall . . . Then she tried to sit in my lap."

(In the film, director Howard Hawks adds: ". . . while I was standing up.")

Later in the book she's a lot less cute. She sucks her thumb and giggles frequently:

> She began to giggle. I put her gun in my pocket and patted her on the back. "Get up, angel. You look like a Pekinese."
>
> She tried to keep a cute little smile on her face but her face was too tired to be bothered.

Later, when she tries to shoot Marlowe,

> her face had the scraped bone look. Aged, deteriorated, become animal, and not a nice animal.

By contrast her older sister, Vivian Regan,

Martha Vickers as Carmen Sternwood in The Big Sleep. *One of Chandler's chillier characters—"Her face had the scraped-bone look. Aged, deteriorated, become animal, and not a nice animal."*
Photofest

was worth a stare. She was trouble . . . I stared at her legs . . . They seemed to be arranged to be stared at . . . The calves were beautiful, the ankles long and slim and with enough melodic line for a tone poem.

Mona Mars (Eddie's wife)—also in *The Big Sleep*—was living proof that appearances are, more often than not, deceptive:
When Marlowe first sees her:

She was so platinumed that her hair shone like a silver fruit bowl . . . It was a smooth silver voice that matched her hair. It had a tiny tinkle in it, like bells in a doll's house. I thought that was silly as soon as I thought about it . . . She brought the glass over. Bubbles rose in it like false hopes.

As, indeed, they should. Her hair was a wig. Marlowe from then on calls her "Silver Wig."

Claire Trevor as Mrs. Grayle/Velma in Farewell, My Lovely. *"She had a full set of curves which nobody had been able to improve on . . . She put her head back and went off into a peal of laughter. I have only known four women in my life who could do that and still look beautiful. She was one of them."* Photofest

Because of Chandler's practice of "cannibalization," we often encounter characters in more than one reincarnation.

We first meet Carmen Sternwood as Carmen Dravec in "Killer in the Rain," where her "white face . . . looked as intelligent as the bottom of a shoe box."

Mrs. Philip Courtney Prendergast appears in "Mandarin's Jade"— "a blonde with black eyes. A blonde to make a bishop kick a hole in a stained-glass window." She is the one who gives private eye John Dalmas the smile he could feel in his hip pocket. Mrs. Prendergast is known to take a drink—or two. She "put her drink to sleep with one punch and looked at the bottle. I milked it again."

" 'Moths in your ermine,' Mrs. Prendergast said, and threw it down the hatch."

In a later encounter, "Her face had, for a brief moment, a sort of half-silly, nymph-surprised-while-bathing expression."

By the time she reappears as Mrs. Grayle (a.k.a. Velma) in *Farewell, My Lovely* she has gained several touches of class, although she still has the ability to drive a bishop to sacrilege:

> Her hair was the gold of gold paintings and had been fussed with just enough but not too much. She had a full set of curves which nobody had been able to improve on . . . She put her head

back and went off into a peal of laughter. I have only known four women in my life who could do that and still look beautiful. She was one of them.

When they are alone, she invites Marlowe to sit beside her on the sofa . . .

"Aren't you a pretty fast worker?" she asked quietly.

I didn't answer her.

"Do you do much of this sort of thing?" she asked with a sidelong look.

"Practically none. I'm a Tibetan monk in my spare time."

"Only you don't have any spare time."

But once again, the passing of time and the plot are not kind to her. When her previous identity as Moose Malloy's girlfriend, Velma, is revealed . . .

her smile became just a little glassy. Suddenly, without any real change in her, she ceased to be beautiful. She looked merely like a woman who would have been dangerous a hundred years ago, and twenty years ago daring, but who today was just Grade B Hollywood.

By the same transformation process Carol Pride in "Mandarin's Jade" becomes Anne Riordan, one of Chandler's few genuine heroines—one of the few women he seems to *like*.

"She was about twenty-eight years old. She had a rather narrow forehead of more height than is considered elegant. Her nose was small and inquisitive, her upper lip a shade too long and her mouth more than a shade too wide. Her eyes were grey-blue with flecks of gold in them [just like Marlowe's]. She had a nice smile. She looked as if she had slept well.

It was a nice face, a face you could get to like. Pretty, but not so pretty that you would have to wear brass knuckles every time you took it out.

A face with bone under the skin, fine drawn like a Cremona violin. A very nice face.

Later Marlowe teases her about her "red hair and her beautiful figure" and is clearly as attracted to her as she is to him. After his drugged encounter with Jules Amthor and his friends, he drags himself to her house for safety. She opens the door . . .

"My God," she wailed. "You look like Hamlet's father!"

As he recovers, Marlowe finds himself softening still more toward her:

"A fellow could settle down here," I said. "Move right in. Everything set for him."
   "If he was that kind of fellow. And if anybody wanted him to," she said.
   "No butler," I said. "That makes it tough."

Lieutenant Randall—like a good cop—can see the way things are, but Marlowe is ready with a riposte . . .

"Not my type . . . I like smooth shiny girls, hardboiled and loaded with sin."
   "They take you to the cleaners," Randall said indifferently.
   "Sure, where else have I ever been?"

Once again the wisecrack preserves him for more of the mean streets.

In *The High Window* we have Linda Conquest, the cabaret singer, another lady with a symbolic name . . .

Her lips seemed to have forgotten to smile. They would smile when she was singing, in that staged artificial smile. But in repose they were thin and tight and angry.

But, more interestingly, we have one of Chandler's damaged ladies—Merle Davis, secretary to Mrs. Murdock . . .

A thin fragile-looking blondish girl in shell glasses . . . She was pale with a sort of natural paleness and she looked healthy enough . . . the whole face had a sort of off-key neurotic charm that only needed some make-up to be striking.

A psychiatrist concludes:

"She'll always be high on nerves and low on animal emotion. She'll always breathe thin air and smell snow. She'd have made a perfect nun . . . As it is she will probably turn out to be one of these acid-faced virgins who sit behind little desks in public libraries and stamp dates in books."

"She's not that bad," Marlowe replies. "And besides, how do you know they are virgins?"

The Little Sister gives us the little sister, Miss Orfamay Quest, ostensibly a simple little girl from Manhattan, Kansas—but with "something in her eyes that was much older than Manhattan, Kansas."

Her steps along the corridor outside made tiny, sharp pecky little sounds, kind of like a mother drumming on the edge of the dinner table when father tried to promote himself a second piece of pie.
      From a strap over her shoulder hung one of those awkward-looking square bags that make you think of a Sister of Mercy taking first aid to the wounded. On the smooth brown hair was a hat that had been taken from its mother too young . . . The rimless glasses gave her that librarian's look.

To begin with, Marlowe doesn't know what to make of her . . .

[She] suddenly began to cry. I reacted to that just the way a stuffed fish reacts to cut bait.

Nancy Guild as Merle Davis in The Brashear Doubloon/The High Window. *"A thin, fragile-looking blondish girl . . . the whole face had a sort of off-key neurotic charm that only needed some make-up to be striking."* Photofest

Later Marlowe is intrigued by this strange little creature enough to want to kiss her:

> I reached up and twitched her glasses off . . . "Without the cheaters those eyes are really something," I said in an awed voice . . . Her upper lids drooped, fluttered a bit and her lips came open a little farther. On them appeared the faint provocative smile that nobody ever has to teach them . . . "Even at the church socials they play kissing games," she said. "Or there wouldn't be any church socials," I said.

Although the other heroine, Mavis Weld, is meant to be the film star (she turns out to be the "little sister's" big sister), easily the most interesting woman is her friend and fellow actor, Dolores Gonzales—"the nicest whore I ever didn't meet," as Chandler describes her.

Marlowe's first encounter is on the phone, and it is not promising . . .

She laughed. I guess it was a silvery tinkle where she was. It sounded like somebody putting away saucepans where I was.

But when he actually meets her: "Sexy was very faint praise for her . . . She looked almost as hard to get as a haircut . . . And exclusive as a mailbox."

"Your name?" Her voice froze on the second word, like a feather taking off in a sudden draft. Then it cooed and hovered and soared and eddied and the silent invitation of a smile picked delicately at the corners of her lips, very slowly, like a child trying to pick up a snowflake . . . She smelled the way the Taj Mahal looks by moonlight . . . She made a couple of drinks in a couple of glasses you could almost have stood umbrellas in.

It rapidly becomes apparent to Marlowe that the lady is "reeking with sex. Utterly beyond the moral laws of this or any other world I could imagine."

She goes into her act . . .

Her shoulders did a fan dance

. . . and before he knows what hit him—

I got out a handkerchief and scrubbed the lipstick off my face. It looked exactly the color of blood, fresh blood.

Every time he is thrown into her company, she throws herself at him. Luckily, Marlowe is used to being slugged and sapped.

I let go of her wrists, closed the door with my elbow and slid past her . . . "You ought to carry insurance on those," I said.

"Just for half an hour," I said, "let's leave the sex to one side. It's great stuff, like chocolate sundaes. But there comes a time when you would rather cut your throat. I guess maybe I'd better cut mine."

Despite the odds, Marlowe survives with his honor intact. "She was one for the book all right."

Exotic and overt as she was, Dolores Gonzalez was never the threat that certain blondes posed.

There are blondes and blondes and it is almost a joke word nowadays. All blondes have their points, except perhaps the metallic ones who are as blonde as a Zulu under the bleach and as to disposition as soft as a sidewalk . . .

"There is the small cute blonde who cheeps and twitters and the big statuesque blonde who straight-arms you with an ice-blue glare. There is the blonde who gives you the up-from-under look and smells lovely and shimmers and hangs on your arm and is always very, very tired when you take her home. She makes that helpless gesture and has that goddamned headache and you would like to slug her except that you are glad you found out about the headache before you invested too much time and money and hope in her. Because the headache will always be there—a weapon that never wears out and is as deadly as the bravo's rapier or Lucrezia's poison vial.

There is the soft and willing and alcoholic blonde who doesn't care what she wears as long as it is mink and doesn't care where she goes as long as it is the Starlight Roof and there is plenty of dry champagne. There is the small perky blonde who is a little pal and wants to pay her own way and is full of sunshine and common sense and knows judo from the ground up and can toss a truck driver over her shoulder without missing more than one sentence out of the editorial in the *Saturday Review*. There is the pale, pale blonde with anemia of some non-fatal but incurable type. She is very languid and very shadowy and she speaks very softly out of nowhere and you can't lay a finger on her because in the first place you don't want to and in the second place she is reading *The Waste Land* or Dante in the original or Kafka or Kierkegaard or studying Provençal. She adores music and when the New York Philharmonic is playing Hindemith she can tell you which one of the six bass viols came in a quarter of a beat too late. I hear Toscanini can also. That makes two of them.

"And lastly there is the gorgeous showpiece who will out-last three kingpin racketeers and then marry a couple of mil-lionaires at a million a head and end up with a pale rose villa at Cap d'Antibes, an Alfa-Romeo town car complete with pilot and co-pilot, and a stable of shopworn aristocrats, all of whom she will treat with the affectionate absentmindedness of an elderly duke saying goodnight to his butler."

—*The Long Goodbye*

And then there was Eileen Wade, the blonde of blondes . . .

Her hair was the pale gold of a fairy princess. There was a small hat on it into which the pale gold hair nestled like a bird in its nest. Her eyes were cornflower blue, a rare color, and the lashes were long and almost too pale.

And when Marlowe hears her speak, she had

a voice like the stuff they used to line summer clouds with.

This is the language of a knight to his lady fair. There is only one small problem. The lady will turn out to be a double murderer.

Marlowe is tempted—as he so often is. Like so many other women he encounters, she is ready to buy him with her body . . .

Underneath it she was as naked as September Morn but a darned sight less coy.

But, as always, he is not for sale. The lady dies and Marlowe lives to fight and, once again, be bloodied but unbowed. Until he meets Linda Loring . . .

She had that fine-drawn intense look that is sometimes neurotic, sometimes sex-hungry, and sometimes just the result of drastic dieting . . . She had very dark eyes. She had the reddest fingernails I had ever seen . . . I put her in the second half of the thirties, early in the second half.

Marlowe meets her in a bar in *The Long Goodbye,* where she is drinking the same rather obscure cocktail, and the exchange is the by now predictable verbal tennis match, at which she more than holds her own . . .

"Perhaps you don't ever make passes at women in bars."

"Not often. The light's too dim."

Why Linda Loring turns out to be *the* woman for Marlowe ends up being one of Chandler's least believable touches. She turns up from time to time but is not really integral to the complex plot, and she is no "smooth shiny girl, hardboiled and loaded with sin." What she is loaded with is money—the daughter of multimillionaire newspaper proprietor Harlan Potter and everything Marlowe despises. She is the one who—not too convincingly—takes his literary virginity and, for once, Marlowe's reaction sounds overemphatic. When she has gone, he goes over to the bed . . .

There was a long dark hair on one of the pillows. There was a lump of lead at the pit of my stomach.

Nina Van Pallandt as Eileen Wade in The Long Goodbye. Photofest

If there were genuine sparks, Chandler didn't manage to convey enough of them to justify Marlowe's sense of loss:

> The French have a phrase for it. The bastards have a phrase for everything and they are always right. To say goodbye is to die a little.

One thing Linda does do for Marlowe is loosen him up a little. After having fought the good but pointless fight, he gives in without a murmur to Miss Vermilyea in *Playback*.

Miss Vermilyea is another platinum blonde, a "very expensive secretary" and, in the words of her boss—who should know—"besides being a lovely piece of female humanity, she's as smart as a whip." After the usual Marlowe exchange she begins to see behind the shabby suit . . .

> "With a little practice I might get to like you. You're kind of cute in a low down sort of way."

. . . and after a brief encounter . . .

> "I hate you . . . Not for this, but because perfection never comes twice and with us it came too soon and I'll never see you again and I don't want to. It would have to be forever or not at all."

By the end of the story he has also succumbed to Betty Mayfield, the woman he has been hired to track . . .

> "Is there some other woman?" she asked softly . . .
> "There have been."
> "But someone very special?"
> "There was once, for a brief moment. But that's a long time ago now."

Later she wonders . . .

> "How can such a hard man be so gentle?"

"If I wasn't hard, I wouldn't be alive. If I couldn't sometimes be gentle, I wouldn't deserve to be alive."

In the early stories women are attracted to Marlowe but have trouble dealing with his essential aloofness. Some of them, like Mavis Weld in *The Little Sister,* attempt to deal with it by putting him down . . .

"What a way you have with the girls . . . It can't be your clothes or your money or your personality. You don't have any. You're not too young, nor too beautiful. You've seen your best days . . ."

A moment later she is kissing him.

The *faux naif* Orfamay Quest teases an answer from him—but it's more from a desire to shock her than a heartfelt revelation. Why had he never married?

"I suppose I know the answer . . . The ones I'd maybe like to marry—well, I haven't what they need. The others you don't have to marry. You just seduce them—if they don't beat you to it."

Good or bad—and anything in between—women are a problem to Marlowe . . .

You can have a hangover from other things than alcohol. I had one from women.

—*The Big Sleep*

Another aspect of the Battle of the Sexes that seemed to give Chandler a headache was the question of the "third sex."

We are now never likely to know whether he was a genuine homophobe or whether his frequent slighting references to homosexuals reflect a prevailing current attitude at a time when alternative sexual preferences were covert and for most people "gay" meant "cheerful." Considering the times, it is surprising how often they appear in the stories, even if most of them are queenly caricatures or dangerous psychopaths.

In *Farewell, My Lovely* Marlowe visits Lindsay Marriott about a possible job . . .

The door opened silently and I was looking at a tall, blond man in a white flannel suit with a violet satin scarf around his neck.

Having examined him carefully, Marlowe concludes . . .

He has the general appearance of a lad who would wear a white flannel suit with a violet scarf around his neck and a cornflower in his lapel.

Later in the book Marlowe visits a bar:

A male cutie with henna'd hair drooped at a bungalow grand piano and tickled the keys lasciviously and sang "Stairway to the Stars" in a voice that had half the steps missing.

On its own it might easily be a cheap crack of no particular significance and with no risk of a Gay Liberation cry of outrage—any more than his aside in *The Big Sleep,* where he referred to "a stealthy nastiness, like a fag party." But this was back in 1940, and by the time of *The Long Goodbye* (1953) the tone is harsher.

Roger Wade complains to Marlowe about the bias of book reviewers. If they thought he was homosexual, he says, they would regard him more favorably:

"Have to take care of their own, you know. They're all queers, you know, every damn one of them. The queer is the artistic arbiter of our age, chum The pervert is the top guy, now."

Four years later Chandler (as Chandler) agrees with him . . .

Perhaps these darling pansies are the symbols of a civilization of the future. If so, let them have it.

—Letter to Michael Gilbert—July 5, 1957

It may be cheap psychiatry to identify Chandler and Marlowe too closely, but it is surely too close to be coincidental that the softening of Marlowe in the later novels so closely parallels Chandler's own mental attitude after the death of Cissy. In the words of the song, they were both "looking for love in all the wrong places."

We leave Marlowe in the fragment of *Poodle Springs* married to Linda and already the cracks are appearing:

> "Damn you, Marlowe, it's not my fault that I'm rich. And if I have the damn money I'm going to spend it. And if you are around some of it is bound to rub off on you. You'll just have to put up with that."
>
> "Yes, darling." I kissed her. "I'll get a pet monkey and after a while you won't be able to tell us apart."

Luckily he didn't live to get the pet monkey . . .

In Marlowe's final short story, "The Pencil" (published in England), he meets Anne Riordan again. She admits her feelings for him but, once again, the knight errant in him comes to his own rescue:

The mature Taki with the mature Chandler at their house in the Pacific Palisades, sometime in the mid-1930s.
Bodleian Library, Oxford

"I'm honest. That's something. But I'm too shop-soiled for a girl like you. I've thought of you, I've wanted you but that sweet clear look in your eyes tells me to lay off . . . I've had too many women to deserve one like you."

The women you get and the women you don't get—they live in different worlds. I don't sneer at either world. I live in both myself.

* * *

TAKI: A PERSONAL INTERPOLATION

"I've been a cat lover all my life (have nothing against dogs except that they need such a lot of entertaining) and have never quite been able to understand them."

Chandler saw himself as a tough guy—someone who could take it and dish it out.

But he had one weakness to which he freely admitted.

Her name was Taki.

Chandler explains his addiction in a letter to Charles Morton on March 19, 1945 . . .

Taki is a black Persian cat, 14 years old, and I call her that because she has been around me since I began to write, usually sitting on the paper I wanted to use or the copy I wanted to revise, sometimes leaning up against the typewriter and sometimes just quietly gazing out of the window from a corner of the desk, as much as to say, "The stuff you're doing's a waste of my time, bud." Her name is Taki (it was originally Take, but we got tired of explaining that this was a Japanese word meaning bamboo and should be pronounced in two syllables), and she has a memory like no elephant ever even tried to have. She is usually politely remote, but once in a while will get an argumentative spell and talk back for ten minutes at a time. I wish I knew what she is trying to say then, but I suspect it all adds up to a very sarcastic version of "You can do better." Taki is a completely poised animal and always knows who likes cats, never goes near anybody that doesn't, always walks straight up to anyone, however lately arrived and completely unknown to her, who really does. She doesn't spend a great deal of time with them, however, just takes a moderate amount of petting and strolls off. She has another curious trick (which may or may not be rare) of never killing anything. She brings 'em back alive and lets you take them away from her. She has brought into the house at various times such things as a dove, a blue parakeet, and a large butterfly. The butterfly and the parakeet were entirely unharmed and carried on just as though nothing had happened. The dove gave her a little trouble, apparently not wanting to be carried around, and had a small spot of blood on its breast. But we took it to a bird man and it was all right very soon. Just a bit humiliated. Mice bore her, but she catches them if they insist and then I have to kill them. She has a sort of tired interest in gophers, and will watch a gopher hole with some attention, but gophers bite and after all who the hell wants a gopher anyway? So she just pretends she might catch one, if she felt like it.

She goes with us wherever we go journeying, remembers all

Ray and Taki at work in La Jolla, c. 1948.
Bodleian Library, Oxford

the places she has been to before and is usually quite at home anywhere. One or two places have got her—I don't know why. She
just wouldn't settle down in them. After a while we know enough
to take the hint. Chances are there was an axe murderer there
once and we're much better somewhere else. The guy might come
back. Sometimes she looks at me with a rather peculiar expression (she is the only cat I know who will look you straight in the
eye) and I have a suspicion that she is keeping a diary, because the
expression seems to be saying: "Brother, you think you're pretty
good most of the time, don't you? I wonder how you'd feel if I
decided to publish some of the stuff *I've* been putting down at
odd moments." At certain times she has a trick of holding one
paw up loosely and looking at it in a speculative manner. My wife
thinks she is suggesting we get her a wrist watch; she doesn't need
it for any practical reason—she can tell the time better than I
can—but after all you gotta have some jewelry.

I don't know why I'm writing all this. It must be I couldn't
think of anything else, or—this is where it gets creepy—am I
really writing it at all? Could it be that—no, it must be me. Say
it's me. I'm scared.

Three years later proper diplomatic relations between cat and
owner have been established. Chandler brings James Sandoe up to
date (September 23, 1948):

Our cat is growing positively tyrannical. If she finds herself alone
anywhere she emits blood curdling yells until somebody comes
running. She sleeps on a table in the service porch and now
demands to be lifted up and down from it. She gets warm milk
about eight o'clock at night and starts yelling for it about 7:30.
When she gets it she drinks a little, goes off and sits under a chair,
then comes and yells all over again for someone to stand beside
her while she has another go at the milk. When we have company
she looks them over and decides almost instantly if she likes them.
If she does she strolls over and plops down on the floor just far
enough away to make it a chore to pet her. If she doesn't like them
she sits in the middle of the living room, casts a contemptuous

glance around, and proceeds to wash her backside. In the middle of this engaging performance she will stop dead, lift her head without any other change of position (one leg pointing straight at the ceiling) stares off into space while thinking out some abstruse problem, then resumes her rear-end-job. This work is always done in the most public manner. When she was younger she always celebrated the departure of visitors by tearing wildly through the house and ending up with a good claw on the davenport, the one that is covered with brocatelle and makes superb clawing, and it comes off in strips. But she is lazy now. Won't even play with her catnip mouse unless it is dangled in such a position that she can play with it lying down. I'm going to send you her picture. It has me in it, but you'll have to overlook that. I believe I told you

April 9, 1948. "I had to hold Taki's tail to keep it still." "Taki" *is another spelling for the Japanese word* Take (bamboo). Photofest

Taki as a kitten, 1932. Chandler described her as "all fur with four legs peeping out from under it."
Bodleian Library, Oxford

how she used to catch all sorts of very breakable living things and bring them in the house quite unhurt as a rule. I'm sure she never hurt them intentionally. Cats are very interesting. They have a terrific sense of humor and, unlike dogs, cannot be embarrassed or humiliated by being laughed at. There is nothing in nature worse than seeing a cat trying to provoke a few more hopeless attempts to escape out of a half-dead mouse. My enormous respect for our cat is largely based on a complete lack in her of this diabolical sadism. When she used to catch mice—we haven't had any for years—she brought them alive and undamaged and let me take them out of her mouth. Her attitude seemed to be, "Well, here's this damn mouse. Had to catch it, but it's really your problem. Remove it at once." Periodically she goes through all the closets and cupboards on a regular mouse-inspection. Never finds any, but she realizes it's part of her job.

Our little black cat had to be put to sleep yesterday morning. We feel pretty broken up about it. She was almost 20 years old. We saw it coming, of course, but we hoped she might pick up strength. But when she got too weak to stand up and practically stopped eating, there was nothing else to do.

All my life I have had cats and I found that they differ almost as much as people . . . Taki had absolute poise, which is a rare quality in animals as well as in human beings. . . . In a group of people she would march straight up to the one cat lover in the room and she would ignore absolutely the occasional individual who was pronouncedly anti-cat. I have never liked anyone who disliked cats, because I've always found an element of acute self-ishness in their dispositions. Admittedly a cat doesn't give you the kind of affection a dog gives you. A cat never behaves as if you were the only bright spot in an otherwise clouded existence. But this is only another way of saying that a cat is not a sentimentalist, which does not mean it has no affection.

But in late 1951 there was something of a happy ending . . .

We have a new black Persian who looks exactly like our last one, so exactly that we have to call him by the same name, Taki.

Eight

Writing (2)
Making Magic

There is a certain quality indispensable to writing from my point of view, which I call magic, but which could be called by other names. It is a sort of vital force.

        —Letter to Jean de Leon—February 11, 1957

Without magic there is no art.

        —Raymond Chandler

In England I am an author. In the USA just a mystery writer.

        —Letter to Paul Brooks—September 28, 1952

To exceed the limits of a form without destroying it is the dream of every magazine writer who is not a hopeless hack.

        —Raymond Chandler

A good story cannot be devised; it has to be distilled.

        —Raymond Chandler

[Literature is] any sort of writing that glows with its own heart.

        —Raymond Chandler

Those who know most about writing are those who can't write.

        —Raymond Chandler

You can't write just because you have read all the books.

—Raymond Chandler

Possibly it was the smell of fear which the stories managed to generate. Their characters lived in a world gone wrong, a world in which, long before the atom bomb, civilization had created the machinery for its own destruction, and was learning to use it with all the moronic delight of a gangster trying out his first machine gun.

—Introduction to *Trouble Is My Business*

The perfect detective story cannot be written. The type of mind which can evolve the perfect problem is not the type of mind that can produce the artistic job of writing.

—"Twelve Notes on the Mystery Story"

I have no theories about writing; I just write. If it doesn't seem to me to be good, I throw it away.

—Letter to Jean de Leon—February 11, 1957

———————

For someone who claimed to have no theories on the subject and whose published output was relatively small, Raymond Chandler wrote a great deal about writing.

Like many writers before him, he believed a certain routine or discipline was essential and when he was in a fit state to write at all, he kept to it religiously. He claimed he spent six hours a day thinking about his writing, four hours writing, four hours reading—too many magazines—six hours sleeping and two hours eating.

There should be a space of time, say four hours a day at least, when a professional writer doesn't do anything but write. He doesn't have to write, and if he doesn't feel like it, he shouldn't try. He can look out of the window or stand on his head or writhe on the floor, but he is not to do any other positive thing,

not read, write letters, glance at magazines, or write checks.
Write or nothing.

—Letter to Alex Barris—March 18, 1949

Chandler himself was a slow, meticulous writer. "I am a fellow
who writes 30,000 words to turn in five," he wrote to Charles Morton
(October 12, 1944):

I work too slowly, throw away too much, and what I write that
sells is not at all the sort of thing I really want to write.

And in an interview with Irving Wallace (August 24, 1945) . . .

I work very fast but I work for the waste basket. I never revise
phrase by phrase and line by line. Instead I rewrite things I don't
like. I work on a typewriter for novels, but at the [film] studio
I dictate. I've written 5,000 words at one sitting, and I always
write the final draft. The faster I write the better my output. If
I'm going slow I'm in trouble. It means I'm pushing the words
instead of being pulled by them . . . I'm a poor plotter and bad at
construction. I never write plots down but work them out in my
head, never completely, but in advance of the words I'm writing.
I'm best when I know my ending, always try to, though I know
intermediate steps.

Chandler was not always completely consistent in his description
of his modus operandi. Only three years later he is telling Mrs. Robert
Hogan (March 7, 1947) . . .

One of my peculiarities and difficulties as a writer is that I won't
discard anything. I can't overlook the fact that I had a reason, a
feeling, for starting to write it, and I'll be damned if I won't lick it.

"I write when I can and I don't write when I can't, always in the
morning or the early part of the day. You get very gaudy ideas at
night but they don't stand up," he told Alex Barris (March 18, 1949).

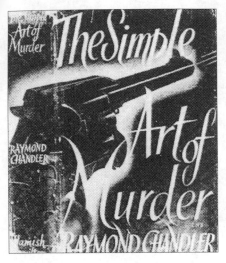

*"In England I am an author.
In the USA just a mystery writer."*

*"I may have written the most
beautiful American vernacular ever
written (some people think I have),
but if it is so, I am still a writer
trying to find his way through a
maze. Should I be anything else?
I can't see it."*

*"I'm an improvisor, and
perhaps at times an innovator."*

*"The test of a writer is whether
you want to read him again years
after he should by the rules be
dated."*

(On another occasion he had explained that he "rarely wrote fiction after dark"—"too ghoulish.") He went on to debate the nature of inspiration . . .

> I'm always seeing little pieces by writers about how they don't ever wait for inspiration; they just sit down at their little desks every morning at eight, rain or shine, hangover and broken arm and all, and bang out their little stint . . . I offer them my admiration and take care to avoid their books.
>
> Me, I wait for inspiration, though I don't necessarily call it by that name. I believe that all writing that has any life in it is done with the solar plexus. It is hard work in the sense that it may leave you tired, even exhausted. In the sense of conscious effort it is not work at all . . .

As the years went by, out went some of the discipline . . .

> I am a spasmodic worker with no regular hours, which is to say I only write because I feel like it. I am always surprised at how easy it seems at the time, and at how very tired one feels afterwards.
> —Letter to Hamish Hamilton—November 10, 1950

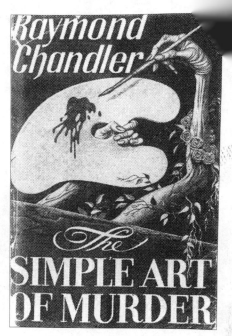

Chandler's definitive essay on crime, "The Simple Art of Murder," was first published in 1943 in The Atlantic Monthly. *In 1950, Houghton Mifflin added other material and published it in hardback form.*

Some of his methods were a little idiosyncratic but they worked for him and provided a necessary focus . . .

I do all my work on yellow paper. Sheets cut in half, typed the long way, triple-spaced. The pages must be from 125 to 150 words and they are so short you don't get prolix. If there isn't a little meat on each, something is wrong.

––October 1, 1957

The character of novelist Roger Wade in *The Long Goodbye* allowed Chandler to write about writing, but also about himself . . .

WADE: In my racket it's so easy to tighten up and get all stiff and wooden. Then the stuff is no good. When it's good it comes easy. Anything you have heard or read to the contrary is a load of mish-mash.

MARLOWE: Depends on who the writer is, maybe. It didn't come easy to Flaubert and his stuff is good.

wade "has made too much money writing junk for halfwits. But the only salvation for a writer is to write. If there is any good in him, it will come out."

No amount of editing and polishing will have any appreciable effect on the flavor of how a man writes. It is the product of the quality of his emotion and perception; it is the ability to transfer these to paper which makes him a writer . . .

—Letter to Mrs. Robert Hogan—March 7, 1947

I do not write . . . for money or prestige, but for love, the strange lingering love of a world wherein men may think in cool subtleties and talk in the language of almost forgotten cultures.

—Letter to Charles Morton—January 15, 1945

When a book, any book, reaches a certain intensity of artistic performance, it becomes literature. That intensity may be a matter of style, situation, emotional tone, or idea, or half a dozen other things.

—Letter to Erle Stanley Gardner—January 29, 1946

From quite early on he was ambivalent about what he was doing:

I no longer have any passion for this stuff. I find myself kidding myself. I enjoy it and find it fun, but I have a suspicion that the quality that finally put these stories over was a sort of controlled half-poetical emotion . . . From the beginning, from the first pulp story it was always with me a question . . . of putting into the stuff something they would not shy off from, perhaps even not know was there as a conscious realization, but which would somehow distill through their minds and leave an afterglow.

—Letter to Alfred Knopf—January 12, 1946

A real writer . . . exists on many levels of thought. Perhaps as a result of my business training I always knew that a writer had to follow a line with which the public would become familiar. He had to "type" himself to the extent that the public would associate his name . . . with a certain kind of writing.

Raymond Chandler

May 21, 1952

Corrections to be made on Copy 1 of THE LONG GOODBYE

✓Page 11, line 3--should read "into the police <u>car</u> and the--"

✓57, second line from end--gr<u>a</u>y suit, not gr<u>e</u>y

✓58, # 3, last line--be sure last sentence is "They chewed my
     tail off." Also second line from end of page--
     "They chewed my tail off." On page 58, line
     2--"They chew your tail off."   59
     (I think all these corrections were made on Copy 1)

✓72, last line--to paste in my scrapbook (not into)

✓73--next to last line--I didn't judge him or analyze hi<u>m</u> (not s)

✓88--Mark letter from Terry to be set in italics--no quotation marks.

✓96--line 12--push buttons should be two words

✓120--line 6--next to last word--change "The way he" to "The <u>road</u> he"

✓147--# 6, line 1--should be Dr. Vujanich

✓154--# 6--should be clothes (not clothese)

✓165 line 4, second word from end of #--should be for not four

✓183--# 2 should end "I shut it again and went back to my desk."
     (Eliminate remainder of #. I think this was done on
     original, but may not be quite correct. Paragraph
     ends as indicated on copy 2, enclosed.

✓191--line 2--word 7, should be here not her. "We never do
     any introducing around here."

✓194--line 2, third word from end of line--I've (not Ive)

✓196--# 7, last word in paragraph should be <u>that</u>. "But how
     could I be sure of that?"

✓232--line five--name is Juan Salvador <u>Garcia</u> de Soto y Sotomayor
     (Add Garcia)

✓233--line 12--last word is hi<u>m</u> (not his)

✓237--# 2, line 12, comma after bronze; line 13 comma after all
     (should be solid bronze, base and all, and heavy.

✓238--line 7--"The mystery was solved." (not They)

✓239--line 8--comma after event. (Should be In the event, I didn't--"

✓244--line 1--last two words should be "What's her" (not What her)
     (This may have been corrected.O

Chandler's corrections for a draft of his sixth novel. Bodleian Library, Oxford

The reading public is intellectually adolescent at best, and it is obvious that what is called "significant literature" will only be sold to this public by exactly the same methods as are used to sell it toothpaste, cathartics and automobiles ... So like all half-educated publics in all ages it turns with relief to someone who tells a story and nothing else. To say that what this man writes is not literature is just like saying that a book can't be any good if it makes you want to read it. When a book, or any sort of book, reaches a certain level of artistic performance, it becomes literature.

—Letter to Erle Stanley Gardner—January 29, 1946

I concentrated on the detective story because it was a popular form and I thought the right and lucky man might finally make it into literature.

—Letter to Wesley Hartley—December 3, 1957

A writer who hates the actual writing, who gets no joy out of the creation of magic by words, to me is simply not a writer at all. The actual writing is what you live for. The rest is something you have to get through in order to arrive at the point.

—Letter to Hamish Hamilton—September 19, 1951

The only thing he could conceive of that would be worse would be "the emptiness of a writer who can't think of anything to write." In a 1951 short story "A Couple of Writers" (published posthumously), he identifies with Hank Bruton ...

"Pastiche," he said drearily. "Everything I write sounds like something a real writer threw away."

Just like a lousy writer, he thought. Never the thing itself, always the cheap emotion that goes with it.

The emptiness was

a pretty painful emptiness, but for some reason it never even approaches tragedy. Jesus, we're the most useless people in the world. There must be a hell of a lot of us too, all lonely, all empty, all poor, all gritted with small mean worries that have no dignity. All trying like men caught in a bog to get some firm ground under our feet and knowing all the time it doesn't make a damn bit of difference whether we do or not ... All the world's would-be writers, the guys and girls that have education and will and desire and hope and nothing else. They know all there is to know about how it's done, except they can't do it. They've studied hard and imitated the hell out of everybody that ever rang the bell.

Too much preoccupation with the mechanics of writing is a sure sign of a weak talent or none at all.

—Letter to Mrs. Robert Hogan—March 8, 1947

I think that certain writers are under a compulsion to write in *recherché* phrases as a compensation for a lack of some kind of natural animal emotion.

—Letter to James Sandoe—April 14, 1949

"Most writers sacrifice too much humanity for too little art."

Thinking in terms of ideas destroys the power to think in terms of emotions and sensations.

—Letter to James Sandoe—December 17, 1944

Oh, the hell with it. Ideas are poison. The more you reason, the less you create.

—Letter to Charles Morton—October 28, 1947

The business of a fiction writer is to recreate the illusion of life. How he does it, if he can do it, it does not in the least help him to know.

—Letter to James Sandoe—December 17, 1944

I don't particularly care for the hard-boiled babies, because most of them are traveling on borrowed gas, and I don't think you have any right to do that unless you can travel a little farther than the man from whom you borrowed the gas.

—Letter to Frederic Dannay—July 10, 1951

Although writing was most certainly Chandler's own personal salvation, he persisted in seeing the dark cloud behind the silver lining. If something was any good, it was, by definition, too good for him . . .

> Everything a writer learns about the art or craft of fiction takes just a little away from his need or drive to write at all. In the end he knows all the tricks and has nothing to say.
> —Introduction to *Trouble Is My Business*

> It has been said, I think, that writers always like the wrong things in their own work.

(A self-fulfilling prophesy he subsequently worked hard to encourage.)

In the early years he was capable of occasional and charming ingenuousness:

> There must be some magic in the writing after all, but I take no credit for it. It just happens, like red hair. But I find it rather humiliating to pick up a book of my own to glance at something, and then find myself twenty minutes later still reading it as if someone else had written it.
> —Letter to Alex Barris—April 16, 1949

By this time his reputation was secure but even fame had its downside in the Chandler scheme of things . . .

> Writers who get written about become self-conscious.
> —Letter to Dale Warren—September 15, 1949

The more things people say about you the more you feel as if you were writing in an examination room, that it didn't belong to you any more, that you had to protect critical reputations and not let them down. Writers even as cynical as I have to fight an impulse to live up to someone else's idea of what they are.

I am so little neglected that I am often actually embarrassed by too much attention.

Defiantly (and self-consciously) he would write Carl Brandt a year later . . .

From now on I am going to write what I want to write as I want to write it. Some of it may flop. There are always going to be people who will say I have lost the pace I had once, that I take too long to say things now, and don't care enough about tight active plots. But I am not writing for those people now. I am writing for the people who understand about writing as an art and are able to separate what a man does with words and ideas from what he thinks about Truman or the United Nations . . .

Style was a constant concern—another by-product of his public school education . . .

The most durable thing in writing is style, and style is the most valuable investment a writer can make with his time. It pays off slowly, your agent will sneer at it, your publisher will misunderstand it, and it will take people you never heard of to convince them by slow degrees that the writer who puts his individual mark on the way he writes will always pay off. He can't do it by trying, because the kind of style I am thinking about is a projection of personality and you have to have a personality before you can project it . . . Preoccupation with style will not produce it.

—Letter to Mrs. Robert Hogan—March 8, 1947

My theory has always been that the public will accept style provided you do not call it style either in words or by, as it were, standing off and admiring it.

—Letter to Bernice Baumgarten—April 16, 1951

Since from the beginning he had been attempting to write

on a level which is understandable to the semi-literate public and at the same time give them some intellectual and artistic over-tones which that public does not seek or demand or, in effect, rec-ognize, but which somehow subconsciously it accepts and likes,"

he had been involved in an ongoing battle with publishers to make them understand what he was trying to achieve artistically. "Would you convey my compliments to the purist who reads your proofs," he wrote to *Atlantic Monthly* publisher Edward Weeks (January 18, 1947) . . .

and tell him or her that I write in a sort of broken-down patois which is something like the way a Swiss waiter talks, and that when I split an infinitive, God damn it, I split it so it will stay split. And when I interrupt the velvety smoothness of a more or less literate syntax with a few sudden words of bar-room vernacu-lar, that is done with the eyes wide open and the mind relaxed but attentive.

The "he or she" turned out to be a she—one Margaret Mutch. When Chandler learned this, he composed a piece of verse to the lady . . .

> Miss Margaret Mutch she raised her crutch
> With a wild Bostonian cry.
> "Though you went to Yale, your grammar is frail,"
> She snarled as she jabbed his eye.
> "Though you went to Princeton, I never winced on
> Such a horrible relative clause!
> Though you went to Harvard, no decent larva'd
> Accept your syntactical flaws.
> Taught not to drool at a Public School
> (With a capital P and S)
> You are drooling still with your shall and will
> You're a very disgusting mess!"

As he "learned" the language Chandler became fascinated by American slang and what he called "hard talk." In his scrapbook he recorded some examples that caught his ear . . .

Chicago lightning—gunfire
Dip the bill—take a drink
Cough yourself off. Be missing . . . beat it
Under glass—in prison, caught
Squibbed off—shot
New Sweet—new girl
Kick the joint—break in
Lip—lawyer
Hard Harry—a hard guy
Pin jabber—hypo user
Dodo—any addict
Daisy crushers—shoes
Kick the gong around—use dope (Harlem)
Caught in a snowstorm—cocained up
Broom—disappear hastily
Put the cross on—mark for death
Back door parole—die in prison

In the early stories he felt obliged to toe the pulp line and pack them with the street jargon he had so laboriously learned. In "Smart-Aleck Kill" alone we find "Drive the heap, bozo!" . . . "It don't listen" . . . "I draw water in this town and I could hang a sign on you" . . . "Light me a pill." In "Nevada Gas": "Are you a guy that can stay clammed?"

And as late as *The Big Sleep*: "Shake some business and pour it. I haven't got all day."

As the years went by and success intruded, Chandler felt he didn't need to try quite so hard with the argot. He dropped a good deal of it and, in any case, as with all "inside" talk, it had passed out of fashion. But for those first few years Los Angeles American really did rival Shakespearean English in its use of the exotic: punk . . . gat . . . butts . . . jake . . . frail . . . powder . . . beef . . . rube . . . grift . . . shamus . . . keester . . . peeper . . . shine . . . pigeon . . .

The literary use of slang is a study in itself. I've found that there are only two kinds that are any good: slang that has established itself in the language and slang that you make up yourself. Everything else is apt to be *passé* before it gets into print.

> —Letter to Alex Barris—March 18, 1949

The lingo varies from place to place, and it also varies from year to year. And there is no doubt that a large part of it is of literary origin . . . Cops and crooks are readers of crime literature, and I have no doubt that many a Western sheriff has ornamented his language and perhaps even his costume from a study of six-gun literature.

> —Letter to Eric Partridge—May 29, 1952

Why is that the Americans—of all people the quickest to reverse their moods—do not see the strong element of burlesque in my writing? Or is it only the intellectuals who miss that?

The question may have been somewhat rhetorical but any card-carrying Brit could have told him the answer. Americans—with few exceptions—have never developed the sense of irony that seems to have been built into the English psyche.

In most ways he was self-aware as a writer and had been from the outset . . .

I have been so belabored with tags like tough, hardboiled, etc., that it was almost a shock to discover occasional signs of almost normal sensitivity in the writing,

he wrote apologetically to his first publisher, Alfred Knopf (February 8, 1942).

On the other hand I did run the similes into the ground.

But by 1948 he is rather proud to claim,

I think I rather invented the trick [of extravagant similes].

Similes and comparisons were Chandler's signature device from the first. In his writer's notebook he kept a list of those that might come in handy, and in *The Long Goodbye* he has alter ego Roger Wade deride it:

Writers. Everything has to be like something else.

It was a preemptive response but a needless one. Everyone who reads him with pleasure is waiting for the next little gem.

The frustrated poet is at work and at home when Chandler observes "a glassed in lounge into which the moonlight poured like water through the floodgates of a dam" (*The Little Sister*) or "a shaft of sunlight tickled one of my ankles" (*The Long Goodbye*).

"The garden hummed with flowers" (*Farewell, My Lovely*) ... the lake "was as motionless as a sleeping cat" (*The Long Goodbye*) ... the shadows were "like crawling lava" (*The High Window*) ... "a wedge of sunlight slipped over the edge of the desk and fell noiselessly to the carpet" (*Farewell, My Lovely*) ... "I stood there, listening to the sunshine burn the grass" (*The High Window*).

Or ... "the elevator rose as softly as mercury in a thermometer" ("Trouble Is My Business") ... "Consciousness evaporated from his eyes" ("Blackmailers Don't Shoot") ... "a few unbeatable wild flowers clawed and hung on [the bank] like naughty children who won't go to bed" ("Mandarin's Jade") ... "The bar entrance was ... dusky and quiet and a bartender moved mothlike against the faint glitter of piled glassware" (*The High Window*) ... "The room was suddenly full of heavy silence, like a fallen cake" (*The Little Sister*) ... "The swell is as gentle as an old lady singing hymns" (*The Long Goodbye*).

He was very sensitive to sound—even the sound of silence ... "The silence held. The room was full of it, brimming over with it. A bird chirped outside in a tree, but that only made the silence thicker.

You could have cut slices of it and buttered them" (*The Lady in the Lake*) . . . Marlowe "opened the door very silently, like snow falling" (*The High Window*) . . . "The minutes went by on tiptoe, with their fingers to their lips" (*The Lady in the Lake*) . . . "The silence fell like a bag of feathers" (*Playback*) . . . "A slug went softly and politely into the parchment-covered wall, high up, making no more sound than a finger going into a glove" ("Mandarin's Jade") . . . "The noise the gun made was no louder than a hammer striking a nail or knuckles rapping sharply on wood" ("Spanish Blood") . . . The car "moved away from the curb and around the corner with as much noise as a bill makes in a wallet" ("Trouble Is My Business") . . . The dollar "went into his pocket with a sound like caterpillars fighting" (*The Lady in the Lake*) . . . "He breathed with a faraway unimportant sound, like distant footfalls on dead leaves" ("Bay City Blues") . . . "making as much noise as a fly makes walking on the wall" (*Farewell, My Lovely*).

Sometimes, of course, the sounds were less soothing . . . "He pushed a cigarette past his lips with a sound like somebody gutting fish" ("Goldfish") . . . "The threshing sound of a telephone being dialed" (*The High Window*) . . . "His words were coming so fast they were leap-frogging themselves" (*Farewell, My Lovely*).

The unusual details of physical appearance invariably caught his questing eye . . .

> A black string tie poked a small hard knot out at the bottom of his collar, like a mouse getting ready to come out of a hole.
> —*The High Window*

> A hand as steady as a stone pier in a light breeze.
> —*The High Window*

> He wore an ascot tie that had been tied about 1880, and the green stone in his stickpin was not quite as large as an apple barrel.
> —*Farewell, My Lovely*

His hat was at least two sizes too small and had been perspired in freely by someone it fitted better than it fitted him. He wore it about where a house wears a wind vane. A tie had apparently been tied with a pair of pliers in a knot the size of a pea.

—*Farewell, My Lovely*

His small neat fingers speared [a cigarette] like a trout taking the fly.

—*Farewell, My Lovely*

A large pleasant-faced man with silvery hair and a dimpled chin and a tiny little mouth made to kiss babies with. He wore a well-pressed blue suit, polished square-toed shoes, and an elk's tooth on a gold chain hung across his stomach . . . He chewed violet-scented breath purifiers.

—"Bay City Blues"

One character was "a piece of gray driftwood carved to look like a man" ("Bay City Blues").

"Old men with faces like lost battles" . . . "He had a wedge-shaped face that ended in a point, like the bottom half of the ace of diamonds" ("Trouble Is My Business") . . . "The upper part of his face meant business. The lower part was just saying goodbye" (*Lady in the Lake*) . . . "His composed gray face was long enough to wrap twice round his neck" (*The Little Sister*) . . . "His chin would never hit a wall before he saw it" (*The Big Sleep*) . . . "He was a tall man with glasses and a high-domed head that made his ears look as if they had slipped down his head" (*The High Window*).

As for the face itself . . . it was "like a gnawed bone" (*The Lady in the Lake*) . . . "as threadbare as a bookkeeper's coat" (*Farewell, My Lovely*) . . . "as intelligent as the bottom of a shoe box" ("Killer in the Rain") . . . "as clear as a cameo" ("Smart-Aleck Kill") . . . "as much expression as a cut of round steak and was much the same color" ("Red Wind") . . . and under pressure it "went to pieces like a clay pigeon" ("Try the Girl") . . . "His face was like a vacant lot" (*The High Window*) . . . "a face like a collapsed lung" (*The Long Goodbye*).

He had "a great deal of domed brown forehead that might at a careless glance have seemed a dwelling place for brains" (*The Big Sleep*) . . . "a dimple in his chin you could have lost a marble in" ("Mandarin's Jade") . . . "one of those moustaches that get stuck under your fingernail" ("Trouble Is My Business") . . . "a few locks of dry white hair clung to his scalp, like wild flowers fighting for life on a bare rock" (*The Big Sleep*) . . . "hair the color of the inside of a sardine can" ("Blackmailers Don't Shoot") . . . "She had weedy hair of that vague color which is neither brown nor blonde, that hasn't enough life in it to be ginger, and isn't clean enough to be grey" (*Farewell, My Lovely*) . . . "pale eyebrows bristling and stiff and round like the little vegetable brushes the Fuller Brush man gives away" (*The Big Sleep*) . . . "A dry, tight, withered smile that would turn to powder if you touched it" (*Farewell, My Lovely*) . . . "[His] eyes popped so far out of his head they looked as if they were on stilts" (*Farewell, My Lovely*) . . . "Her lips rustled like tissue-paper" (*Farewell, My Lovely*) . . . "Her hair was as artificial as a night club lobby" (*The High Window*) . . . "a couple of eyebrows . . . they waved gently, like the antennae of some suspicious insect" (*The Long Goodbye*).

Nor did matters improve lower down his face . . .

The eyes were "the color of a drink of water" (*The Lady in the Lake*) . . . "dirty ice" (*The Long Goodbye*) . . . "as simple as forest water" ("I'll Be Waiting") . . . "the lifeless glitter of thick ice" ("I'll Be Waiting") . . . "as dead as stale oysters" ("Blackmailers Don't Shoot") . . . "Her eyes became narrow and almost as black and shallow as enamel on a cafeteria tray" . . . they "snapped very wide open, like seeds bursting from a pod" ("Nevada Gas") . . . and he had "a stare that would have frozen a fresh-baked potato" (*The Long Goodbye*) . . . "He had two expressions—hard and harder" (*Playback*) . . . "He had eyes the color of a drink of water" ("The Lady in the Lake"—short story).

His smile was "as stiff as a frozen fish. His long pale hands made gestures like sick butterflies over the top of his desk" ("The Man Who Liked Dogs") . . . "a dry, tight, withered smile the lips have forgotten before they reach the eyes" (*The Big Sleep*) . . . "a nice smile—like an alligator" ("The Curtain") . . . "the sort of smile the operating room sees" (*The Big Sleep*) . . . It "hung from the corners of his mouth like cobwebs in the corners of an old ceiling." ("Bay City Blues") . . . "He smiled—call it a down-payment on a smile" (*Playback*).

He had a nose "like a straphanger's elbow" (*The Little Sister*) . . .

And as for the mouth . . . it was "a mouth made for three-decker sandwiches" ("Red Wind") . . . "He had a mouth a dentist could have got both hands in, up to the elbows" ("The Man Who Liked Dogs") . . . "His mouth looked like a black pit and his breath came in little waves, choked, stopped, came on again, limping" ("Red Wind") . . . "He grinned widely with as many teeth as a horse" ("Red Wind") . . . "He had beautiful teeth but they hadn't grown in his mouth" ("Finger Man").

"Her teeth had the nice shiny look that comes from standing all night in a glass of solution" (*Farewell, My Lovely*) . . . "He grinned. His teeth had a freckled look" ("Red Wind") . . . "He grinned. His dentist was tired of waiting for him" ("The Pencil") . . . "The smile fell off his face like a soiled rag" (*Farewell, My Lovely*).

And the voice that came out . . . "a dry voice. You might even call it parched" (*The High Window*) . . . "a toneless voice, flat as a piece of slate" (*The Lady in the Lake*) . . . "a soft voice, soft and dry, like the rustle of well-worn leather" ("The Curtain") . . . "thin and dry and rustled like bamboo leaves" (*Playback*) . . . "a voice as silky as a burnt crust of toast" ("Red Wind") . . . "The mellow voice of a circus barker" . . . "a voice like old ivory ("Guns at Cyrano's") . . . "a hushed voice, like a six-hundred dollar funeral" (*The Little Sister*) . . . "a voice the size of a marble" (*The Lady in the Lake*) . . . "hoarse and awkward, like a rusty lock . . . a voice that could have been used for paint remover" (*The Little Sister*) . . . "used to split firewood" . . . "a voice as hard as the blade of a shovel" (*The Lady in the Lake*) . . . "the voice was still as a breadstick" (*The Big Sleep*) . . . "as cool as boarding house soup" (*The Little Sister*) . . . "as cool as a cafeteria dinner" (*Farewell, My Lovely*) . . . "a voice that grew icicles" . . . "The big man purre softly, like four tigers after dinner" (*Farewell, My Lovely*) . . . "a voice you could have cracked a Brazil nut on" (*The Lady in the Lake*).

It was . . . "fat. It wheezed softly, like the voice of a man who had just won a pie-eating contest" ("Trouble Is My Business) . . . It "faded off into a sort of sad whisper, like a mortician asking for a down payment" (*The Little Sister*) . . . "Thick and clogged, as if it was being strained through a curtain or somebody's long white beard" (*The Little Sister*) . . . It "dragged itself out of her throat, like a sick man getting out of bed" (*Farewell, My Lovely*) . . . "like a convalescent rooster learning to crow again after a long illness" (*The High Window*) . . . "something like a very large and very old dog barking" ("Bay City Blues") . . . "I left her laughing. The sound was like a hen having hiccups" (*Farewell, My Lovely*) . . . "He snorted and his nostrils got very wide. They had been wide enough for mouseholes to start with" (*Farewell, My Lovely*) . . . "She laughed without making any more sound than you would make cracking a bread stick" (*Farewell, My Lovely*).

And before a few more lines had passed, it "screamed like a dozen sheets tearing" ("Bay City Blues").

"He talked the way New Yorkers used to talk before they learned to talk Flatbush" (*The Long Goodbye*) . . . "It is so long since I heard anyone talk the way Jane Austen writes" ("Pearls Are a Nuisance").

As you look at his imagery, certain themes emerge. Animals abound: "I flicked the blackjack at his wandering hand. It drew into itself, like a slug on a hot stone" ("The Man Who Liked Dogs") . . . "Fat spiders slept behind the windows like bishops" ("English Summer") . . . "An hour crawled by like a sick cockroach" (*The Long Goodbye*) . . . He felt "as cold as a frog, as green as the back of a new dollar bill" (*Farewell, My Lovely*) . . . "a Charvet scarf you could have found in the dark by listening to it purr" (*The Little Sister*) . . . "The brown man screamed thinly, like a hungry kitten" ("Spanish Blood") . . . "The thunder was tumbling about in the hills, like a bunch of elephants playing tag" ("The Curtain") . . . "The lake was as motionless as a sleeping cat" (*The Long Goodbye*).

Of all the animal kingdom, he seemed to have a marked preference for fawns: "She jerked away from me like a startled fawn might, if I had a startled fawn and it jerked away from me" (*The Little Sister*) . . . "Her breath was as delicate as the eyes of a fawn" (of Mona Mars in *The Big Sleep*) . . . and the lake in *Lady in the Lake* is called Fawn Lake . . .

Sometimes the animal imagery is transferred, as in "The barman scuttled around, hating us with the whites of his eyes" ("Try the Girl").

Or else "He looked at me, like a stone lion outside the Public Library" ("Mandarin's Jade") . . . "The big man looked at me as if I had just hatched out" (*Farewell, My Lovely*) . . . "crazy as a pair of waltzing mice" ("Killer in the Rain").

Even when it's inanimate, it's more often harsh than not. The perfume was "elderly . . . like three widows drinking tea" (*The Lady in the Lake*) . . . "His face was like a vacant lot" (*The High Window*).

The plot had "all the originality and drive of a split fingernail" (*The High Window*) . . . "as gaudy as a chiropractor's chart" (*The Little Sister*) . . . "He waved a generous hand on which a canary-yellow diamond looked like an amber traffic light" (*The Little Sister*) . . . "A nice sense of humor—like a morgue attendant" (*Farewell, My Lovely*).

The occasional softer image is allowed to intrude: "I pushed [the door] open with the tenderness of a young intern delivering his first baby" (*The Little Sister*) . . . "She shut the door . . . as carefully as if it was made of short pie crust" (*Farewell, My Lovely*) . . . "the perfume shop with its rows of delicately lighted bottles, ranged like the ensemble in the finale of a Broadway musical" ("Guns at Cyrano's") . . . "He fluttered around making elegant little gestures and body movements as graceful as a Chopin ending" (*The Little Sister*).

Or an ironic one: "a garage as easy to drive into as an olive bottle" ("Try the Girl") . . . "thin as an honest alibi" (*The High Window*) . . . "tasteless as a roadhouse blonde" ("Spanish Blood") . . . "The walls here are as thin as a hoofer's wallet" (*Playback*) . . . "He was as neat as a gift book" ("Mandarin's Jade") . . . "It felt like shaking hands with a towel-rack" (*The Lady in the Lake*).

The topic of *time* seemed to inspire: "Another army of sluggish minutes dragged by" (*The Big Sleep*) . . . "For all of a minute—which in a spot like that can be as long as a chiropractor's thumb" (*The Lady in the Lake*) . . . "The minutes dropped silently down a well" (*The Little Sister*) . . . "The passing minutes seemed to fall into a void, with a soft whirring sound, like spent rockets" (*The Long Goodbye*).

And, as Marlowe would say, "Always the wisecrack where possible": "A man you can't kid is a man you can't trust" (*The Lady in the Lake*) . . . "He's so tight his head squeaks when he takes his hat off" ("Trouble Is My Business") . . . "The only difference between you and a monkey is you wear a larger hat" . . . "He looked like a man who could be trusted with a secret—if it was his own secret" (*The High Window*) . . . "Take your ears out of the way and I'll leave" . . . "Dead men are heavier than broken hearts" (*The Big Sleep*) . . . "He's the fellow for whom they coined the phrase, 'as ignorant as an actor' " (*The High Window*).

And the Groucho-esque "If you don't leave, I'll get somebody who will."

In the same way that Chandler "cannibalized" some of his short stories to form the basis of his early novels, he would rework certain of his favorite similes. It's interesting to see how he honed them.

Sometimes they were simple variations on a theme: "He shut his mouth as if a winch controlled it" ("The Curtain") . . . "He shut his mouth with all the deliberation of a steam shovel" ("The Man Who Liked Dogs").

"He looked about as unobtrusive as a tarantula on a slice of angel food cake" (*Farewell, My Lovely*) becomes "I belonged in Idle Valley like a pearl onion on a banana split" (*The Long Goodbye*) . . . "As easy to spot as a kangaroo in a dinner jacket" (*Playback*).

Or . . .

"As a bluff mine was thinner than the gold on a weekend wedding ring" ("Finger Man") becomes "His surprise was as thin as the gold a weekend wedding band" (*The Long Goodbye*).

But sometimes the changes are subtler. In "Try the Girl" the cop "looked poor and sour and honest" but in *Farewell, My Lovely* he looked "poor enough to be honest."

"Her giggles ran around the room like rats" ("Killer in the Rain"). In *The Big Sleep* they . . . "ran around the corners of the room like rats behind the wainscoting"—somehow a more evocative image.

The scene in which Marlowe first meets General Sternwood in *The Big Sleep* is an excellent example of Chandler shaping his material. In the original scene in "The Curtain," Carmady (the pre-Marlowe private eye) is told by General Winslow, "Take your coat off, sir . . . Orchids require heat, Mr. Carmady—like rich old men." By *The Big Sleep* it has become "You may take your coat off, sir. It's too hot in here for a man with blood in his veins." The difference being that we now know what sort of man this "rich old man" used to be, and how he now lives what is left of his life through others.

> The old man licked his lips watching me, over and over again, like an undertaker dry-washing his hands.

There were, of course, times when—as he himself was aware—he was prone to "run the similes into the ground" . . .

> A hush that would have made a Southern senator sound like a deaf mute asking for a second plate of mush.
> —"Bay City Blues"

> He looked as nervous as a brick wall.
> —*Farewell, My Lovely*

> His smile was as faint as a fat lady at a firemen's ball.
> —*The High Window*

> He had brilliant eyes that wanted to look hard, and looked as hard as oysters on the half-shell.
> —*Farewell, My Lovely*

The wet air was as cold as the ashes of love.

—*Farewell, My Lovely*

She looked as flustered as a side of beef.

—*The High Window*

I was about as much use as a hummingbird's spare egg would have been.

—*The High Window*

On the dance floor half a dozen couples were throwing themselves around with the reckless abandon of a night watchman with arthritis.

—*Playback*

The General spoke again, slowly, using his strength as carefully as an out-of-work showgirl uses her last good pair of stockings.

—*The Big Sleep*

A small radio that was as full of static as the mashed potato was full of water.

—*The Lady in the Lake*

"I could use a five dollar bill so rough Abe Lincoln's whiskers would be all lathered up with sweat."

—*The High Window*

. . . he said softly, in the manner of a sultan suggesting a silk noose for a harem lady whose tricks have gone stale.

—*"Mandarin's Jade"*

The purring voice was now as false as an usherette's eyelashes and as slippery as a watermelon seed.

—*The Big Sleep*

I go limp as a scrubwoman's back hair.

> —"Pearls Are a Nuisance"

She was as limp as a fresh-killed rabbit.

> —*Farewell, My Lovely*

"This car sticks out like spats at an Iowa picnic."

> —"Mandarin's Jade"

He had a heart as big as one of Mae West's hips.

> —*Farewell, My Lovely*

He had as much charm as a steel puddler's underpants.

> —*The Long Goodbye*

The [TV] commercials would have sickened a goat raised on barbed wire and broken beer bottles.

> —*The Long Goodbye*

The house was leaking guests out of the evening air . . . goodbyes were bouncing around like rubber balls.

> —*The Long Goodbye*

He was as calm as an adobe wall in the moonlight.

> —*The Long Goodbye*

A hat that had been taken from its mother too young.

> —*The Little Sister*

He came back softly . . . debonair as a French count in a college play.

> —*Farewell, My Lovely*

Just as he uses Los Angeles as a character in his stories, he uses buildings. His descriptions key in the mood . . .

The Rossmore Arms was a gloomy pile of dark red brick built around a huge forecourt. It had a plush-lined lobby containing silence, a bored canary in a cage as big as a dog-house, a smell of old carpet dust and the cloying fragrance of gardenias long ago.

—The Lady in the Lake

. . . and even the weather plays a bit part . . .

That semi-desert where the sun is as light and dry as old sherry in the morning, as hot as a blast furnace at noon, and drops like an angry brick at nightfall . . . the air's stale before it gets up in the morning.

—The Lady in the Lake

Chandler was in love with words to the point of being besotted by them. When he ventured into fantasy fiction—a form that intrigued him enough for him to contemplate giving up the "hard-boiled stuff" to concentrate on it—the words betrayed him and he self-indulgently overwrote.

For him the detective form was ideal. It allowed him to use language exotically but within a tight discipline—one that he did much to refine over the years:

Detective stories should be about the detective first and the story second.

It is the pace that counts, not the logic or the plausibility, or the style.

It is a dream world which may be entered and left at will, and it leaves no scars.

His kind of story was at a far remove from the "classic" form, one that he distrusted intuitively . . .

[It isn't] possible to write a strictly honest mystery of the classic type . . . To get the complication you fake the clues, the timing, the play of coincidence, assume certainties where only 50 per cent chances exist at most. To get the surprise murderer you fake character, which hits me hardest of all, because I have a sense of character . . . for Christ's sake, let's not talk about honest mysteries. They don't exist.

> —Letter to George Harmon Coxe—June 27, 1940

The detective or mystery story as an art form has been so thoroughly explored that the real problem for a writer now is to avoid writing a mystery story while appearing to do so.

> —Letter to James Sandoe—January 26, 1944

Time—and greater experience—did nothing to dilute his skeptical view:

The novel of detection little by little educates the public to its own weaknesses, which it cannot possibly remove, because they are inherent. It can flourish only until enough people know its vocabulary.

> —Letter to James Sandoe—October 2, 1947

I really don't seem to take the mystery element in the detective story as seriously as I should . . . the mind which can produce a coolly-thought-out puzzle can't, as a rule, develop the fire and dash necessary for vivid writing.

> —Letter to Charles Morton—July 17, 1944

Murder novels . . . they have the elements of heroism without being heroic . . . border on tragedy and never quite become tragic . . . it is possible that the tensions in a novel of murder are the simplest and yet most complete pattern of the tensions in which we live in this generation.

> —Letter to James Sandoe—October 18, 1948

The role of mystery novelist, he felt, was "to outwit the reader without out-thinking him" ("The Simple Art of Murder"—1950).

At least half the mystery novels published violate the law that the solution, once revealed, must seem to be inevitable.

I have suspected for some time that the better you write a mystery, the more clearly you demonstrate that the mystery is really not worth writing . . . If it is well written, it shouldn't be a mystery.
—Letter to Hamish Hamilton—October 5, 1949

The mystery writer's material is melodrama, which is an exaggeration of violence and fear beyond what one normally experiences in life . . . The means he uses are realistic in the sense that such things happen to people like these and in places like these; but this realism is superficial; the potential of emotion is overcharged, the compression of time and event is an improbability, and although such things happen, they do not happen so fast and in such a tight frame of logic to so closely knit a group of people.
—Letter to Bernice Baumgarten—March 11, 1949

The mystery story is a kind of writing that needs not dwell in the shadow of the past and owes little if any allegiance to the cult of the classic . . . There are no "classics" of crime and detection. Not one. Within its frame of reference, which is the only way it should be judged, a classic is a piece of writing which exhausts the possibilities of its form and can hardly be surpassed. No story or novel of mystery has done that yet. Few have come close. Which is why otherwise reasonable people continue to assault the citadel.
—"The Simple Art of Murder" (1950)

In a later letter (to Bernice Bergman, May 14, 1952) he pursued the point . . .

I don't care whether the mystery was fairly obvious but I cared about the people, about this strange corrupt world we live in, and how any man who tries to be honest looks in the end either sentimental or just plain foolish . . . You write in a style that has been imitated, even plagiarized, to the point where you begin to look as if you were imitating your imitators.

In any case, most of those imitators missed the point by confusing violence with content:

The best hardboiled writers never try to be tough; they allow toughness to happen when it seems inevitable for its time, place and condition.

—Letter to Dorothy Gardner—January 1956

From early in his career it irked him to be lumped in with

the smooth and shallow operators like [Ngaio] Marsh, [Rex] Stout and [Agatha] Christie. Very likely they write better mysteries than I do, but their words don't get up and walk. Mine do . . .

—Letter to Hardwick Moseley—April 23, 1949

I am not just a tough writer; I am the best there is in my line and the best there has ever been; I am tough only incidentally; substantially I am an original stylist with a very daring kind of imagination.

—Letter to Carl Brandt—December 21, 1950

Although in 1955 he is telling Hamish Hamilton (April 27) that he is

just a beat-up pulp writer and that in the USA is ranked slightly above a mulatto.

A thriller writer in England, if he is good enough, is just as good as anyone else.

Nonetheless . . .

I still regard myself as an amateur and insist on having some fun out of my work. I just can't take myself seriously enough to be otherwise.

In *The Lady in the Lake* Marlowe parodies the kind of story in which he himself had his beginning. He tells murderess Muriel Chess, who is menacing him,

"Detective confronts murderer. Murderer produces gun, points same at detective. Murderer tells detective the whole sad story, with the idea of shooting him at the end of it. Thus wasting a lot of valuable time, even if in the end murderer did shoot detective. Only murderer never does. Something always happens to prevent it."

And again . . .

The time comes when you have to choose between pace and depth of focus, between action and character, menace and wit. I now choose the second in each case.

—Letter to Alex Barris—April 16, 1949

In 1949 he decided it was time to set down a few ground rules for his chosen form of expression. He called them "Casual Notes on the Mystery Novel" and they read (in part) . . .

1. The mystery novel must be credibly motivated both as to the original situation and the denouement. It must consist of the plausible actions of plausible people in plausible circumstances, it being remembered that plausibility is largely a matter of style.
2. The mystery story must be technically sound about methods of murder and detection.
3. It must be realistic as to character, setting and atmosphere. It must be about real people in a real world.
4. The mystery novel must have a sound story value apart from the mystery element.
5. The mystery novel must have enough essential simplicity of structure to be explained easily when the time comes.
6. The mystery must elude a reasonably intelligent reader.
7. The solution, once revealed, must seem to have been inevitable.
8. The mystery novel must not try to do everything at once.
9. The mystery novel must punish the criminal in one way or another, not necessarily by operation of the law courts.
10. The mystery novel must be reasonably honest with the reader.

There were several addenda . . .

1. The perfect mystery cannot be written.
2. It has been said that "nobody cares about the corpse." This is nonsense, it is throwing away a valuable element. It is like saying that the murder of your aunt means no more to you than the murder of an unknown man in a city you never visited.
3. A mystery serial seldom makes a good mystery novel. The curtains depend for their effect on your not having the next chapter. When the chapters are put together the moments of false suspense are merely annoying.
4. Love interest nearly always weakens a mystery because it introduces a type of suspense that is antagonistic to the detective's struggle to solve the problem.
5. It is the paradox of the mystery novel that while its structure will seldom if ever stand up under the close scrutiny of an analytical mind, it is precisely to that type of mind that it makes its greatest appeal.
6. Show me a man or woman who cannot stand mysteries and I will show you a fool, a clever fool—perhaps—but a fool just the same.

People will continue to read mysteries. Maybe because regular novels are no longer satisfying as stories. Or maybe it's the inner sadism in people. Or maybe Somerset Maugham is right that everyone is fascinated by mysteries because murder is the one irrevocable crime. You can get back the jewels, but never a human being's life.
—Interview with Irving Wallace—July 1946

Over time he realized that changing times and tastes would force a change in the genre . . .

The hard-hitting story will not die completely but it will have to become more civilized.

By 1953 he is writing to Alfred Knopf . . .

I'm a little tired of the kick-'em-in-the-teeth stuff myself. I hope I have developed, but perhaps I have only grown tired and soft, but certainly not mellow.

What a pity there is nothing in essay writing. I could have been a very fine essayist, and should thoroughly have enjoyed that. Much more so than murder stories, which part of my mind always looks on with a certain condescension.

—Letter to Juanita Messick—August 12, 1953

Heigh ho, I think I'll write an English detective story, one about Superintendent Jones and two elderly sisters in the thatched cottage, something with Latin in it and music and period furniture and a gentleman's gentleman: above all one of those books where everybody goes for nice long walks.

—Letter to Blanche Knopf—October 22, 1942

The passing of the years did nothing to improve matters. He would complain to Hamish Hamilton . . .

I'm fed up with the California locale . . . There are things about writing that I love, but it is a lonely and ungrateful profession and personally I'd much rather have been a barrister, or even an actor.

—January 16, 1954

Dame Agatha Christie
(1890–1976). Photofest

One of the many foreign-language editions. This one started life as "Spanish Blood."

Two years later the place is even more to blame . . .

I know now what is the matter with my writing or not writing. I've lost my affinity for my background. Los Angeles is no longer my city . . . There is nothing for me to write about. To write about a place you have to love it or hate it or do both by turns, which is usually the way you love a woman. But a sense of vacuity or boredom—that is fatal.

—Letter to Jessica Tyndale—July 12, 1956

Tough and cynical as he chose to appear, Chandler never took his eye off posterity and frequently hinted at his own literary epitaph— occasionally striking a note of the *faux naïf* in doing so that he despised when he detected it in others . . .

What greater prestige can a man like me (not too greatly gifted, but very understanding) have than to have taken a cheap, shoddy

and utterly lost kind of writing, and have made of it something
that intellectuals claw each other about?

—Letter to Charles Morton—January 15, 1945

In his letters he would externalize the ceaseless internal debate . . .

What should a man do with whatever talent God happened in
an absent moment to give him? Should he be tough and make a
lot of money like me? . . . A writer has nothing to trade with but
his life . . . So how much do you concede? I don't know. I could
write a best-seller, but I never have. There was always something I
couldn't leave out or something I had to put in . . .

I am not a dedicated writer. I am only dedicated as a person . . .
Most writers are frustrated bastards with unhappy domestic lives.
I was happy for too long a time, perhaps. I never really thought
of what I wrote as anything more than a fire for Cissy to warm
her hands at. She didn't even much like what I wrote. She never
understood, and most people don't, that to get money you have
to master the world you live in, to a certain extent, and not be too
frail to accept its standards.

In this same letter to John Houseman, he added, as a sort of
valediction . . .

I hope you know I never thought of myself as important and
never could. The word itself is even a bit distasteful.

I suppose all writers are crazy, but if they are any good, I
believe they have a terrible honesty.

—Letter to Edgar Carter—June 3, 1957

It was for others to reach the verdict he wanted. In its obituary the
London *Times* concluded . . . "In working the common vein of crime
fiction he mined the gold of literature."

Nine

Envoi

A Long Goodbye . . . to the Big Sleep

What did it matter where you lay once you were dead? In a dirty sump or in a marble tower on top of a high hill. You were dead, you were sleeping the big sleep, you were not bothered by things like that. You just slept the big sleep, not caring about the nastiness of how you died or where you fell.

—*The Big Sleep*

We still have dreams, but we know now that most of them will come to nothing. And we also most fortunately know that it really doesn't matter.

—Letter to Charles Morton—October 9, 1950

It is one of the [few] charms of not being as young as you were that you can stick your neck out, because you don't give a damn.

My salute to posterity is a thumb to the end of the nose and the fingers outspread.

There is no trap so deadly as the trap you set for yourself.

—*The Long Goodbye*

"Time makes everything mean and shabby and wrinkled. The tragedy of life . . . is not that the beautiful things die young, but that they grow old and mean."

—Roger Wade in *The Long Goodbye*

To know me in the flesh is to pass on to better things.

I think I might be the first to admit that the sort of reticence which prevents a man from exploiting his own personality is really an inverted sort of egotism.

—Raymond Chandler

Raymond Chandler lived several lives in parallel.

There was the Raymond Chandler that other people saw, living, sometimes only partly living, breathing, eating—and frequently drinking. Quiet, studious and courteous when sober; quarrelsome and curmudgeonly when drunk.

Personally I am sensitive and even diffident. At times I am extremely caustic and pugnacious, at other times very sentimental. I am not a good mixer because I am very easily bored, and to me the average never seems good enough, in people or in anything else.

—Letter to Hamish Hamilton—November 10, 1950

I am one of those people who have to be known exactly the right amount to be liked. I am standoffish with strangers, a form of shyness which whiskey cured when I was still able to take it in the requisite quantities. I am terribly blunt, having been raised in that English tradition which permits a gentleman to be almost infinitely rude if he keeps his voice down.

My character is an unbecoming mixture of outward diffidence and inward arrogance.

I am not a completely amiable character any more than I am a facile and prolific writer. I do most things the hard way, and I suffer a good deal over it.

I am, as a matter of fact, rather a supercilious person in many ways. I shouldn't be at all surprised if it shows in what I write.

I never sulk. I am never huffy. Sometimes, I admit, I can be pretty irritable, but this is perhaps more the fault of a nervous temperament than of any innate vice.

There was the Raymond Chandler of the copious correspondence. Reflective, introspective, reaching out to anyone who would answer and play pen pal. The letters—as someone said—were "the conversations of a lonely man."

"You got a friend somewhere who might like to hear your voice?" Marlowe asks rhetorically in *The Little Sister.*

I don't know why I write so many letters. I guess my mind is just too active for my own good . . . It's true that in letters I sometimes seem to have been more penetrating than in any other kind of writing . . . as I re-read some of them, I am really astonished . . . at the facility of expression and the range of thought I seemed to show even when I was only a struggling beginner . . .

Some are analytical, some are a bit poetical, some sad, and a good many caustic or even funny. They reveal, I suppose, a writer's reaction to his early struggles and later his attempts to ward off the numerous people who exploit him in some way.

—Letter to Hamish Hamilton—May 16, 1957

I have too much in me that never gets a chance to get said. It's probably not worth saying but then that doesn't help me to realize that.

I'm afraid this letter may seem to you too personal. If so, may you forgive me? Sometimes I feel terribly alone.

—Letter to Edward Weeks—February 27, 195-

Then there was Chandler-as-Marlowe—the tough, incorruptible man who saw society's flaws, accepted them with a wry shrug and a slug of booze and rose above them. For much of his professional life Marlowe was his ideal self, and the identification became so total that it was sometimes difficult to know who was talking—even though Chandler himself liked to deny it.

As Chandler's life began to unravel, Marlowe softened, too.

> Something inside me had gone sour . . . No feelings at all was exactly right. I was as hollow as the spaces between the stars.
>
> —*The Long Goodbye*

In and of itself it was an incestuous process and a story that should have been written—by someone else.

Finally, there was Chandler–as–Roger Wade—the self-destructive,

The Long Goodbye. *Hamish Hamilton, London, 1953.*

loquacious writer. The bad Chandler. As Marlowe began to rust around the edges, like a knight in armor that's been left out in the rain one time too many—as Chandler might have said, though better—Chandler found a new home for his increasing sourness and cynicism in the character of Wade, who briefly spars with Marlowe in *The Long Goodbye.*

In an earlier book Wade would have provided the opportunity for Chandler to take a more or less objective swing at literary pretension. Here he is not so much writing about writers as about himself: "He was a weak man, unreconciled, frustrated, but understandable."

Chandler-Marlowe, however, can see a glimmer of hope. He tells Mrs. Wade that, despite all his faults, Wade is "a guy who can take a long hard look at himself and see what is there. It's not a very common gift. Most people go through life using up half their energy trying to protect a dignity they never had."

Maybe, but the good side of Wade is easy to miss in print and in the end even Marlowe had had enough . . .

> Roger Wade is dead . . . He was a bit of a bastard and maybe a bit of a genius, too. That's over my head. He was an egotistical drunk and he hated his own guts. He made me a lot of trouble and in the end a lot of grief. Why the hell should I be sympathetic?

It was the kind of epitaph Chandler might have written about himself: "It's as if I had two natures, one good, one bad."

"He was a good actor," Eileen Wade says of her late husband. "Most writers are."

And Chandler admitted to Natasha Spender, a friend of later years,

> I have an endless sense of the dramatic that I never seem to play any part quite straight. My wife always says I should have been an actor.

And to another friend . . .

> "All the rest [has] been play-acting."

Late-life loves. Helga Greene: Chandler met her in England in 1955. She became his agent in the late 1950s and also his fiancée. Her father disapproved of their intended marriage and Chandler died soon afterward. She inherited his estate. (Chandler is wearing gloves to cover a skin condition.)

The letters certainly give an impression of someone striving to shape a public persona and not entirely sure of the character he is trying to create. What does seem clear is that Chandler was increasingly writing for posterity. ("To hell with posterity. I want mine now!"—1947)

While frequently disclaiming their importance, he nonetheless sounded out his British publisher, Hamish Hamilton, on the feasibility of publishing his letters at some point. Certainly, he had kept copies.

> When I have done what passes for a day's work, I am sucked dry. I have nothing to say in the damn letters. I start them but don't finish them. I have a box file stuffed with carbon copies . . . Gosh, what a lot I had to say, and on the whole how well I said it. Now it is becoming a bit of an effort to say anything. I am only too well aware that I have said it all before and said it better.
>
> —Letter to Charles Morton—October 9, 1949

Natasha Spender (1919–2010): Chandler wanted to marry her but there was one small snag. She was already married to the English poet Stephen Spender.

As his output of fiction declined, so the volume of letters increased. *Quid pro quo?* By this time he was in his sixties and under severe stress. After Cissy died he lived, by his own admission, "a posthumous life." Friends, he came to believe, could be "a fire against the darkness"—though he was not particularly skilled or consistent in tending the fire.

Apart from his observations on the writer's lot, much of what he wrote to his very varied correspondents was about his own state of mind . . .

She was the beat of my heart for thirty years. She was the music heard faintly at the edge of sound. It was my great and now useless regret that I never wrote anything really worth her attention, no book that I could dedicate to her. I planned it. I thought of it, but I never wrote it. Perhaps I couldn't have written it . . . I regarded the sacrifice of several years of a rather insignificant literary career as a small price to pay, if I could make her smile a few times mor

—Letter to Leonard Russell—December 29, 1

Cissy was gone but she never left him . . .

I try not to think too much about Cissy. Late at night when people have gone to bed and the house is still and it is difficult to read I hear light steps rustling on the carpet and I see a gentle smile hovering at the edge of the lamplight and I hear a voice calling me by a pet name. Then I go out to the pantry and mix a stiff brandy and soda and try to think of something else.

—Letter to Hamish Hamilton—January 22, 1955

I'm going to fill the house with red roses and have a friend in to drink champagne, which we always did. A useless and probably a foolish gesture, because my lost love is so utterly lost and I have no belief in any after life. But just the same I shall do it. All us tough guys are sentimentalists at heart.

—Letter to Roger Machell—February 7, 1955

As the months passed the need to be in love grew . . .

Right now I'd like to sleep with almost any pretty soft gentle woman, but of course I shan't do it (even if I had the chance), because there has to be love. Without that it is nothing . . . because I loved her so much that now she is gone I love all gracious and tender women.

—Letter to Helga Greene—June 19, 1956

Greene was by now his agent and, just before Chandler died, had agreed to marry him. On July 13 he continued the line of thought.

I knew so little about women . . . I know almost too much now. And yet I have never become cynical about them, never ceased to respect them, never for a moment failed to realize that they face hazards in life which a man does not face, and therefore should be given a special tenderness and consideration . . . This feeling which I have about women which women obviously do not feel about themselves . . . Women are so damn vulnerable to all sorts hurts.

The thought of marriage recurred constantly. He wrote to Jessica Tyndale ("a girl I have not even seen") in August of that year . . .

> I really don't want to get married again because my heart was in too many places and a wife would never have more than a part of me.

A year later . . .

> I suppose that a man who was married for almost 31 years to a woman he adored becomes in a sense a lover of all women, and is forever seeking, even though he does not know it, for something he has lost.
>
> —Letter to Edgar Carter—June 3, 1957

In the end, death decided the debate.

Chandler appears to have had no real political agenda apart from a total distrust of power in any form and a more general philosophy of life, picked up at an early age, that the whole business was "today a pat on the back, tomorrow a kick in the teeth."

As the later years dragged by—and despite his assertion that he had "no belief in any after life"—he became more reflective about what, if anything, came next:

> The older you get, the less you know.
>
> —Letter to Deirdre Gartrell, July 25, 1957

In his last novel, *Playback,* two of his several self-portraits engage in a debate of sorts. Marlowe is asked by Henry Clarendon, an old man close to death . . .

> "Do you believe in God, young man?"
>
> "If you mean an omniscient and omnipotent God who intended everything exactly the way it is, no."
>
> "But you should, Mr. Marlowe. It is a great comfort. We a'

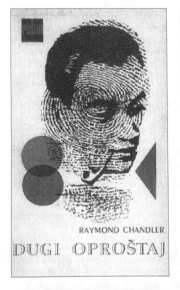

RAYMOND CHANDLER

DUGI OPROŠTAJ

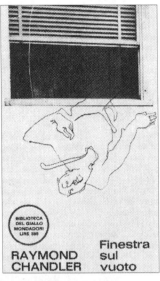

BIBLIOTECA
DEL GIALLO
MONDADORI
LIRE 350

**RAYMOND
CHANDLER**

**Finestra
sul
vuoto**

Raymond Chandler

**IL GRANDE
SONNO**

EDIZIONE INTEGRALE

LIRE
250

MONDADORI

GYLDENDALS FLAGGERMUSBØKER

**DEN LANGE
SØVNEN**

Skjebnen slår lettsindig familie.

Chandlerworld: The Long Goodbye *(in Serbo-Croatian);* The High
Window *(Italy);* The Big Sleep *(Italy);* The Big Sleep *(Norway).*

come to it in the end because we have to die and become dust. Perhaps for the individual that is all, perhaps not. There are grave difficulties about the afterlife. I don't think I should really enjoy a heaven in which I shared lodgings with a Congo pygmy or a Chinese coolie or a Levantine rug peddler or even a Hollywood producer. I'm a snob, I suppose, and the remark is in bad taste. Nor can I imagine a heaven presided over by a benevolent character in a long white beard locally known as God. These are foolish conceptions of very immature minds. But you may not question a man's religious beliefs however idiotic they may be. Of course, I have no right to assume that I shall go to heaven. Sounds rather dull, as a matter of fact. On the other hand how can I imagine a hell in which a baby that died before baptism occupies the same degraded position as a hired killer or a Nazi death-camp commandant or a member of the Politburo? How strange it is that man's finest aspirations, dirty little animal that he is, his finest actions also, his great and unselfish heroism, his constant daily courage in a harsh world—how strange that these things should be so much finer than his fate on this earth. That has to be somehow made reasonable. Don't tell me that honor is merely a chemical reaction or that a man who deliberately gives his life for another is merely following a behavior pattern. Is God happy with the poisoned cat dying alone in convulsions behind the billboard? Is God happy that life is cruel and that only the fittest survive? The fittest for what? Oh no, far from it. If God were omnipotent and omniscient in any literal sense he wouldn't have bothered to make the universe at all. There is no success where there is no possibility of failure, no art without the resistance of the medium."

Clarendon—and perhaps Chandler, too—had predicted in some detail how the game was likely to end . . .

The starched white dragons will minister to me. The bed will be wound up, wound down. Trays will come with that awful loveless hospital food. My pulse and temperature will be taken at frequent intervals and invariably when I am dropping off to sleep. I shall

*Chandler shortly before
his death, 1959.*

lie there and hear the rustle of starched skirts, the slurring sound
of rubber shoe soles on the aseptic floor, and see the silent horror
of the doctor's smile. After a while they will put the oxygen tent
over me and draw the screens around the little white bed and I
shall, without even knowing it, do the one thing in the world no
man ever has to do twice.

What he felt at the end is a matter of surmise.

Raymond Thornton Chandler died on March 26, 1959.

t was not a dramatic ending and perhaps the cynic in him would
ve found that appropriate, since he was never convinced that he
s entitled to what he had. The five-year "posthumous life" he lived
r Cissy's death had proved a burden to him and his friends. A

halfhearted suicide attempt had thrown him back into the embrace of his significant other—alcohol.

He chose to see Helga Greene as his last lifeline, and they planned to marry. Chandler stayed sober to meet her father but when it became clear that he met with no favor in that quarter, he let go of the lifeline. As far as he could see, there was nothing left to live for. But what was so surprising about that?

"I have lived my whole life on the edge of nothing," he wrote to his English lawyer, Michael Gilbert (July 25, 1957).

The fact that we are still thinking and writing about him more than half a century later surely indicates that in this, at least, he was wrong.

Angel's Flight, Bunker Hill. Courtesy Estate of William Reagh

Permissions and Thanks

I am grateful to the RAYMOND CHANDLER ESTATE for permission to quote from Chandler's fiction and letters and to reproduce illustrations from the Chandler Archive held in Oxford's Bodleian Library . . . in particular to Graham Greene, CBE, Ed Victor and Sarah Williams.

. . . to the staff of the BODLEIAN . . . in particular Colin Harris, Superintendent of the Department of Special Collections.

. . . to HAMISH HAMILTON for permission to reproduce their dust jacket designs for Chandler's U.K. editions.

. . . to ALFRED A. KNOPF for permission to reproduce their original book jackets.

. . . to DULWICH COLLEGE—Chandler's *alma mater*—for permission to publish the views of the college . . . in particular Calista Lucy, Keeper of the Archive.

. . . to PHOTOFEST for never failing to come up with just the picture you had in mind . . . in particular Howard and Ron Mandlebaum.

. . . to CRAIG TENNEY of Harold Ober Associates Inc. for permission to reproduce James M. Cain's letter to Chandler after *Double Indemnity*.

. . . and especially to my publisher, VICTORIA WILSON, who, over the years, has learned how—politely but firmly—to keep me on track!

And, as always, my agent and friend, ALAN BRODIE.

—BARRY DAY
2014

Index

Page numbers in *italics* refer to illustrations.

Academy, xi, 10
Academy Awards (Oscars), xiv, 31, 144
Adams, Cleve, 35–6
Adrian, Jean (char.), 168
African Americans, Los Angeles and, 116
Alfred A. Knopf, xiii, xiv, *38, 39*
Allen, Frederick Lewis, xvii
American English, 25–6
Amthor, Jules (char.), 41, 82, 176
Anthony, Bruno (char.), 160–1
Arcadia, Calif., xiii
Archer, Lew (char.), *101*
Archer, Miles (char.), *101*
Ashenden (Maugham), 33, 34
Atlantic Monthly, xiv, 126, 130, 140, *197,*
    204

Babcock, Dwight, *24*
Bacall, Lauren, *42,* 145, 152, 153, *165*
Ballard, W. T., *24*
Barnes, Arthur, *24*
Barris, Alex, 19, 23, 195, 202, 206
Baumgarten, Bernice, 81, 203, 220
"Bay City," xiii, 88, 92, 94, 96, 118–20, *119*
"Bay City Blues" (Chandler), xiii, 46, 69,
    77, 96, 148, 150, 166, 169, 208, 209, 211,
    212, 215
Beerbohm, Max, 12
Beifus (char.), 95
Bendix, William, 146
Bethel, Jean, 140
Beulah (char.), 165

Big Sleep, The (Chandler), *45, 46,* 48, 49, 50,
    56, 59, 60, 61, 79, 185, 227
    chess in, 44–5
    cops in, 91, 93
    foreign editions of, *236*
    Geiger in, 28, 167
    Hollywood in, 147, 148, 151
    Los Angeles in, 102, *104,* 109, *117*
    Marlowe's beating in, 74, 76
    Marlowe's ethics in, 41, 63
    Marlowe's office in, 51, 52
    Marlowe's pragmatism in, 67
    Marlowe's smoking in, 73
    Marlowe's wit in, 68, 70
    publication of, 38, *39*
    reviews of, 39, 47
    Sternwood Mansion in, *44*
    women in, 166, 167, 168, 172–3, 184
    writing process of, xiii, 37, 40, 205, 209,
        210, 211, 213, 214, 215, 216
Big Sleep, The (film), xiv, *42,* 145, 151–5, *154,*
    165, 173
Billy Wilder in Hollywood (Zolotow), 130
"Blackmailers Don't Shoot" (Chandler), xii,
    23, 24–5, 27, 44, 115, *165,* 207
Black Mask, xii, *xii,* xiv, 23, *24,* 25, 27, 44,
    47, 127
Blue Dahlia, The (film), xiv, *128,* 140–5, *141,*
    142, 143, 151, 155
Bogart, Humphrey, *42,* 145, 152, 153, 154
Bond, James (char.), 153
Brackett, Leigh, 154

Brandt, Carl, 203, 221
Brasher Doubloon, The (film), xiv, *178*
Breeze, Lieut. (char.), 88, 97
British Columbia Regiment, *13*
Brody, Joe (char.), *104*, 147
Brooks, Paul, 27, 193
Bruton, Hank (char.), 200
Butler, John K., *24*

Cahuenga Building, *105*
Cain, James M., xiv, xviii, 28, *28*, 30–1, 127, 131, *132*, *133*
California, Chandler's arrival in, *15*, 16
Camel cigarettes, 53, *54*
Canadian Expeditionary Force, xi
Canadian Gordon Highlanders, *12*, 13–14
Carmady (char.), 46, 215
Carter, Edgar, 226, 235
"Casual Notes on the Mystery Novel" (Chandler), 222–3
Chandler, Cissy Pascal, xi–xii, 17–18, *17*, *19*, *21*, 37, 118–19, 121, 156, 163, 226, 233–4
    death of, xiv, 81, 82, 186, 239
Chandler, Florence Thornton, 4, *5*, 6, 15, *15*, 17
Chandler, Maurice, 4, 6
Chandler, Raymond, *16*, *46*, *101*
    Adams and, 35–6
    Alfred Knopf and, xiii, xiv, 12, 37, 38–40, 156–7, 198, 206, 223
    Allen and, xvii
    Arcadia and, xiii
    awards and honors of, xiv, 31, 144, 162
    Barris and, 19, 23, 195, 202, 206
    Baumgarten and, 81, 203, 220
    Bethel and, 140
    "big sleep" phrase and, 35–6
    birth of, xi, 3, 4
    Blanche Knopf and, 31, 40, 109, 224
    Blue Dahlia screenplay of, xiv, *128*, 140–5, *143*, 151, 155–6
    Brandt and, 203, 221
    Brooks and, 27, 193
    Cain and, xiv, xviii, 28, 30–1, 127, 131, *132*, *133*
    Carter and, 226, 235
    cat (Taki) and, *186*, 187–92, *188*, *190*, *191*
    in Chicago, 4
    childhood and youth of, xi, xvii–xviii, 4–9, *5*, *6*, *8*, *9*
    chronology of, xi–xv
    Cissy Pascal and, xi–xii, xiv, 17–18, *17*, 37, 81, 82, 118–19, 121, 156, 163, 186, 226, 233–4, 239
    civil service and, 9–10
    Coxe and, 37, 38, 120–1, 135, 219

Cypress Grove and, *15*
Dannay and, 201
death of, xv, 238, *238*
de Leon and, 193, 194
Depression and, 17, 18
    Double Indemnity screenplay of, 127–31, *128*, *129*, *132*, *133*, 152
    drinking of, xii, xiv, xv, 18, 55, 143–4, 163, 228, 239
    education of, xi, xviii, 6–9, *7*, *8*, 203
    England and, xi, xiv, xv, 3, 6–9, *7*, *8*, 10–13, 20
    European sojourn of, 9–10, *9*, *10*, 13
    fantasy fiction and, 36–7, 218
    film industry and, xiii, xiv, 31, 79, 125–62, *128*, *129*, *132*, *133*, 195
    first story of, xii
    Fitzgerald and, 32–3
    Gardner and, 25, 28, 29–30, 136, 198, 200
    Gartrell and, 14
    Gilbert and, 86, 170–1, 185, 239
    Guinness and, 82, 83
    Hamilton and, xvii, 4, 13, 16, 18, 21, 24, 27, 33, 36, 37, 38, *64*, 80, 123, 126, 135, 136, 153, 157, 161–2, 196, 200, 220, 221, 224, 228, 229, 232, 234
    Hammett and, xviii, *24*, *26*, 28–9, 30, 31, 46, 47, *101*, 135
    Hartley and, 10, 27, 200
    Hawks and, 152, 153, 154–5, *154*, 172
    health of, xiv, xv
    Helga Greene and, xv, 28, 123, 162, *232*, 234, 239
    Hemingway and, xviii, 30, *30*, 31–2, 48
    Hersey and, 20, 157
    Higgins and, 20
    Hitchcock and, xiv, 157–61
    homosexuals and, 184–5
    Houghton Mifflin and, xiv
    Houseman and, 24, 43, 140–4, 163–4, 226
    Howard and, 25
    Ibberson and, 43
    in Ireland, 6, *6*
    Karloff and, 9
    in La Jolla, xiii, xiv, xv, 121–2, *121*, 156, *188*
    Lake and, 145, *164*
    language and, xviii, 19, *22*, 23–7
    lawyers and, 98
    letter writing and, 229, 232–3
    Los Angeles and, *see* Los Angeles, Calif.
    Machell and, 41, 79, 234
    Marlowe and, *see* Marlowe, Philip (char.)
    marriage certificate of, *21*
    Maugham and, 33–4, 223
    McDermid and, 158
    Messick and, 224

money and, 94–5, 98–9, 105
in Monrovia, xiii
Morgan and, 13
Morton and, 5, 6, 11, *30*, 127, 135, 142–3,
    187–9, 195, 198, 201, 219, 226, 227, 232
Moseley and, 221
mother and, 4, *5*, 6, 15, *15*
Mrs. Hogan and, 195, 198, 200–1, 203
Mutch and, 204
Mystery Writers of America and, xv
in Nebraska, 5
in New York, xv
obituary of, 226
Offord and, 139
oil industry and, xii, 17–18, *22*
O'Neill and, 35–6
Partridge and, 206
personality of, 228–9
on police and crime, 85–99
religion and, 4, 6, 235–8
Roger Wade and, 230–1
romances of, 231, *232*, *233*, 234, 235, 239
Russell and, 233
Sanders and, 37
Sandoe and, 20, 35, 71, 77–8, 144–5,
    189–91, 201, 219
in Santa Monica, xiii, 118–19
sense of home as lacking in, 3–18
Spender and, 231, *233*
suicide attempt of, 239
Swanson and, 127, 146
tax problems of, xv
Tyndale and, 83, 123, 225, 235
Wallace and, 195, 223
Warren and, 25, 33, 78, 125, 126, 134, 138,
    202
Weeks and, 138, 204, 229
Wilder and, xiv, 31, 127–30, *129*
Wodehouse and, 9
women and, 163–84, *173*, 186–7
World War I and, xi, *12*, 13–15, *13*, *14*
World War II and, 144–5
see also writing
chess, 44–5, 61–2
Chess, Muriel, 221
Chicago, Ill., 4
Chiozza, Dolores (char.), 165
Christie, Dame Agatha, xviii, 221, *224*
Christy-French, Lieut. (char.), 89–90
cigarettes, 53, *54*, 73
Civil Service, British, Chandler and, 9–10
Clarendon, Henry (char.), 235–7
coffee, 60, *61*
Conquest, Linda (char.), 147, 176
Conrad, Joseph, 24
Continental Op (char.), 46

Conversations with Wilder (Crowe), 128, 130
cops, 85–99, *91*
"Couple of Writers, A" (Chandler), 200
Coxe, George Harmon, 37, 38, 120–1, 135,
    219
"Critical Notes" (Chandler), 137
"Curtain, The" (Chandler), xii, 37, 46, 109,
    211, 214, 215
Cypress Grove, Calif., *15*

Dabney Oil Syndicate, xii, 22
Dalmas, John (char.), *xiii*, 43–4, 46, 166
Dannay, Frederic, 201
Davis, Bette, 147, *148*
Davis, Merle (char.), 177, *178*
Davis, Norbert, *24*
Degarmo, Lieut. (char.), 91
de Leon, Jean, 193, 194
deMille, Cecil B., 146
Depression, Great, 17, 18, 108
Detective Fiction Weekly, 27
Dickens, Charles, 29
Dime Detective, *xii*, xiii, *xiii*, 27
Dionne Quintuplets, 52, *53*, 57
Dmytryk, Edward, 153
Donovan, Carol (char.), 170
Double Indemnity (Cain), xiv, 31, 131, *132*,
    133
Double Indemnity (film), xiv, 31, 127–31, *128*,
    129, *130*, *132*, *133*, *134*, 152, 161
Doyle, Sir Arthur Conan, 80
Dravec, Carmen (char.), 174
Dulwich College, xi, 6–9, *7*, *8*
Dumas, Alexandre, 29

Endicott, Sewell (char.), 95
England, Chandler and, xi, xiv, xv, 3, 6–9, *7*,
    8, 10–13, 20
"English Summer" (Chandler), 212
Evans, John (char.), 46, 65

Falcon Takes Over, The (film), xiii, 152
Famous Players-Lasky, *128*
Farewell, My Lovely (Chandler), 41, 48, 51, 57,
    59, 63, 65, 66, 73, 82, 118–19, 185
cops in, 85, 92, 93, 94–5, 96, 97
Hemingway and, *30*, 32, 94
Los Angeles in, 102, 103, 109, 111, 113, 116
Marlowe's wit in, 49, 69, 70, 71
publication of, xiii
reviews of, 47
women in, 168, 169, 171, 174–6, *174*
writing of, 207, 208, 209, 210, 211–12, 21⁻
    214, 215, 216, 217
Farewell, My Lovely (film), *152*, *174*
Farr, Rhonda (char.), 165

Faulkner, William, 154
film industry, *110*, *155*
    Chandler and, xiii, xiv, 31, 79, 125–62, *128*,
    129, *132*, *133*, 195
    Marlowe and, 139–40, 147, 151, 152–3, 154,
    155, *155*, 156
"Finger Man" (Chandler), xii, 55, 60–1, 211,
    214
Fitzgerald, F. Scott, 32–3, *33*
Fitzgerald, Zelda, *33*
Fleming, Ian, 153
Florian, Jessie (char.), 171
Fortnightly Intruder, 34
Four Roses, 54
"Free Verse" (Chandler), 11
Fromsett, Adrienne (char.), *169*
Furthman, Jules, 154

Gardner, Dorothy, 29, 221
Gardner, Erle Stanley, 25, 28, 29–30, *29*, 136,
    198, 200
Gartrell, Diedre, 14
Geiger (char.), 28, 167
Germany, Chandler and, 9–10, *10*
Gilbert, Michael, 86, 170–1, 185, 239
Glass Key, The (film), *141*
"Goldfish" (Chandler), xii, 50, 71, 170, 208
Goldwyn, Samuel, 156
Gonzales, Dolores (char.), 32, 178–80
Granger, Farley, *158*
Grant, Cary, 43, 153
Grayle, Mr. (char.), 48
Grayle, Velma (char.), 116, 169, 174, *174*, 175
Greene, Helga, xv, 28, 123, 162, *232*, 234, 239
Greer, Lieut. (char.), 92
Gregorius, Capt. (char.), 91
Gregory, Capt. (char.), 91, 93
Greystone Mansion (Beverly Hills,
    Calif.), *44*
Guild, Nancy, *178*
Guinness, Maurice, 82, 83
"Guns at Cyrano's" (Chandler), xii, 168, 211,
    213

Haines, Guy (char.), 160–1
Haines, Miriam (char.), 160
Hamilton, Hamish, xvii, 4, 13, 16, 18, 21, 24,
    27, 33, 36, 37, 38, *64*, 80, 123, 126, 135,
    136, 153, 157, 161–2, 196, 200, 220, 221,
    224, 228, 229, 232, 234
Hamish Hamilton (publishing company),
    45, *230*
[H]ammett, Dashiell, xviii, *24*, *26*, 28–9, 30,
    31, 46, 47, *101*, 135
[Har]tley, Wesley, 10, 27, 200
[Hea]wood, Joyce (char.), *141*

Hawks, Howard, 152, 153, 154–5, *154*, 172
Hecht, Ben, 159
Hemingway, Ernest, xviii, 30, *30*, 31–2, 48
"Hemingway" (char.), 32, 94
Henreid, Paul, 147, *148*
Hersey, John, 20, 157
Higgins, George V., 20
High Sierra (film), 153
High Window, The (Chandler), xiv, 41, 42, 51,
    53, 62, 63, 65, 84, 128
    chess in, 62
    cops in, 88, 97
    Hollywood in, 139, 147, 149, 152
    Italian edition of, *236*
    Los Angeles in, 105, 110, *113*, 114
    Marlowe's loneliness in, 76
    Marlowe's smoking in, 74
    Marlowe's wit in, 68, 69, 70, 71, 72
    women in, 166, 167, 169, 170, 171, 176–7
    writing of, 207, 208, 209, 210, 211, 212, 213,
    214, 215, 216
High Window, The (film), *178*
Hitchcock, Alfred, xiv, 140, 157–61, *158*
Hogan, Mrs. Robert, 195, 198, 200–1, 203
Hollywood, Calif., 102, 125–62, *125*
    Paramount's Bronson Gate in, *128*
    Schwab's Pharmacy in, *150*
    Walk of Fame in, 162
    see also Los Angeles, Calif.
"Hollywood and the Screen Writer"
    (Chandler), 156
Holmes, Sherlock (char.), 80
homosexuality, 184–5
Houghton Mifflin, xiv, *197*
Houseman, John, 24, 43, 140–4, *142*, 163–4,
    226
Howard, James, 25
Huggins-Young coffee, 60, *61*
Huntress, Harriet (char.), 165–6
Hurlburt, Pearl Eugénie Pascal, *see* Chandler,
    Cissy Pascal
Hutton, Betty, 146

Ibberson, D. J., 43
Iceman Cometh, The (O'Neill), 35
"I'll Be Waiting" (Chandler), xiii, 210
Ireland, Chandler in, 6, *6*

Karloff, Boris (William Henry Pratt), 9
"Killer in the Rain" (Chandler), xii, 37, 46,
    174, 209, 213, 215
"King in Yellow, The" (Chandler), xiii, 109,
    114, 165
Knopf, Alfred, xiii, xiv, 12, 37, 38–40, *38*,
    156–7, 198, 206, 223
Knopf, Blanche, 31, *38*, 40, 109, 224

Ladd, Alan, 140, *141*, 144, 145, 146
"Lady in the Lake, The" (Chandler), 76, 210
Lady in the Lake, The (Chandler), xiv, *45*, 50,
   57, 59, 65, 74, 119–20, *119*
   cops in, 85–6, 88, 90, 91, 92, 97
   Los Angeles in, 100
   Marlowe's loneliness in, 77
   women in, 169
   writing of, 207–8, 209, 210, 211, 212, 213,
   214, 216, 218
Lady in the Lake, The (film), 50, 155, *155*, *169*
La Jolla, Calif., xiii, xiv, xv, 121–2, *121*, 156,
   188
Lake, Fawn (char.), 213
Lake, Veronica, *141*, 145, *164*
Lennox, Terry (char.), 54–5
Little Sister, The (Chandler), 42, 48, 49, 53,
   58, 63–4, *64*, 66, 69, 70, 71, 73, 77, 79,
   83, *119*, 229
   cops in, 85, 89–90, 95, 96, 99
   Hemingway and, 32
   Hollywood in, 126, 139–40, 146, 148, 149,
   151
   Los Angeles in, 101, 105, 106, *108*, 109, *112*,
   113, 115, 116–18, 122, 126
   publication of, xiv
   women in, 167–8, 169, 171, 177–80, 184
   writing of, 207, 209, 211, 212–13, 214, 217
London, England, Chandler and, xi, xiv, xv,
   3, 6–9, *7*, *8*, 10–13, 20
London *Times*, 226
Long Goodbye, The (Chandler), 32, 49, *54*, 57,
   59, 60, *61*, 62, 64, 65, 67, 73, 79, 227, *230*
   chess in, 62
   cops in, 86, 90, 91, 93, 94, 95, 96, 98
   Hollywood in, 137, 146–7, 149–50, 151
   Los Angeles in, 101, 109, *122*, 123–4
   Marlowe's changed character in, 80, 81,
   82, 84
   Marlowe's drinking in, 54–5
   Marlowe's loneliness in, 76, 77
   organized crime in, 86, 98
   publication of, xiv
   rich people in, 78
   Roger Wade in, 20, 42, 185, 197–8, 207,
   228, 230–1
   Serbo-Croatian edition of, *236*
   women in, 70, 167, 170, 180–3, *182*
   writing of, 197–8, *199*, 207, 209, 210, 212,
   214, 217
Long Goodbye, The (film), *182*
Loring, Linda (char.), 57, 60, 76, 79, 82,
   181–3, *186*
Los Angeles, Calif., xii, xviii, 3, *4*, 100–24,
   100, *102*, *122*, 225
   African Americans in, 116

Ambassador Hotel in, *106*
architecture of, 11, 102–3, *103*, *113*, 114,
   217–18
Beverly Hills Hotel in, *110*
Beverly Hills in, 106, 111
in *The Big Sleep*, 102, *104*, 109, *117*
Brown Derby restaurant and, 102, *106*,
   107
Bunker Hill and, *113*, 114
Cahuenga Building and, *105*
Chandler and, xii, xviii, 3, *4*, 105, 108, 109,
   111, 114, 115–16, 118, 120–1, 123, 146, 225
City Hall in, *108*
in *Farewell, My Lovely*, 102, 103, 109, 111,
   113, 116
film industry in, *110*, 126
Grauman's Chinese Theatre in, 102, *103*
Hollywood Boulevard in, *103*, *105*, 150
Hollywood in, 102, *106*, 146
Hotel Tremaine in, 115
in *The Little Sister*, 101, 105, 106, *108*, 109,
   112, 113, 115, 116–18, 122, 126
in *The Long Goodbye*, 101, 109, *122*, 123–4
neon lights in, 106, 109, *112*, 113
oil industry and, 107
organized crime in, 93–4, 107
population growth in, 107
Richfield Building in, *112*
Santa Ana winds in, 112
smog in, 123
Studio City in, 118
Sunset Boulevard in, *117*, 118
Van Nuys Hotel in, 115
Ventura Boulevard in, 118
Vine Street in, *107*
Westwood in, *106*
Wilshire Boulevard in, *104*, 106, *106*
World War II and, 107–8
Lozelle, "Blonde Agnes" (char.), 167, 168

Macdonald, Ross, 101, *101*
Machell, Roger, 41, 79, 234
MacMurray, Fred, *129*, *134*
Mafia, 98–9
   see also organized crime
Mallory (char.), 44, 83
Malloy, Moose (char.), 116, 175
Malory, Thomas, 44
Maltese Falcon, The (film), 140, 153
Maltese Falcon, The (Hammett), 46
"Mandarin's Jade" (Chandler), *xii*, 43–4, 46,
   103, 105, 115, 149, 166, 170, 174, 175, 207,
   208, 210, 213, 216, 217
Mansion House Hotel, 58–9
"Man Who Liked Dogs, The" (Chandler),
   xii, 46, 100, 210, 211, 212, 214

Marlowe, Philip (char.), *xiii*, xviii, 32, 41–84, *42*, *52*, *119*, *152*, 229, 231
  Anne Riordan and, 98, 175–6, 186–7
  apartments of, *58*, 60–1, 62
  art and, 49
  biography of, 47–8
  calendars and, 57–8
  cars and, 55–7, *56*
  Chandler's creation of, xiii, 40
  Chandler's identification with, 47–8, 78, 79, 80, 186, 230, 231
  changes in, 79–82, 84, 186
  chess and, 44–5, 61–2
  clichés and, 73
  cops and, 85–99
  drinking by, 54–5, *61*, 62
  film industry and, 139–40, 147, 151, 152–3, 154, 155, *155*, 156
  firearms and, 55, *56*
  food and, 59–60, *61*
  homosexuals and, 185
  Linda Loring and, 57, 60, 76, 79, 82, 181–3, 186
  loneliness of, 76–7
  Los Angeles and, 49–50, 109, 115, 122, 123–4; *see also* Los Angeles, Calif.
  marriage and, 82–4
  money and, 63–5, 94–5, 98–9
  offices of, 51–2, *52*, 57–9
  Ohls as alter ego of, 97–9
  organized crime and, 86, 93–4, 98–9
  physical description of, 50–1
  pragmatism of, 67–8
  predecessors to, 43–4, 46
  professional ethics of, 41, 63, 65–7, 86–8
  religion and, 235, 237
  rich people and, 78–9
  smoking by, 53–4, *54*, 73–4
  social conscience of, 78–9
  wit and wisecracks of, 49, 68–72, 214
  women and, 70, 79, 154, 166–84, 186–7
  on writing and storytelling, 197, 208, 221–2
Marr, Belle (char.), 165
Marriott, Lindsay (char.), 185
Mars, Eddie (char.), 70, 93–4, 173
Mars, Mona (char.), 173, 213
Marsh, Ngaio, 221
Marshall, George, 143
Matson, Helen (char.), 166
Maugham, W. Somerset, 33–4, *34*, 223
Mayfield, Betty (char.), 183
McCoy, Horace, *24*
McDermid, Finley, 158
McKim, Tod (char.), 91
Menendez (char.), 82

Messick, Juanita, 224
MGM, xiv, 127, 155–6
Millar, Kenneth (Ross Macdonald), 101, *101*
Moffatt, Raymond T., *24*
Monrovia, Calif., xiii
Montgomery, Robert, *50*, *52*, *155*, 156
Morgan, Neil, 13
Morny, Mrs. (char.), 166, 167, 169
Morte d'Arthur (Malory), 44
Morton, Charles, 5, 6, 11, *30*, 127, 135, 142–3, 187–9, 195, 198, 201, 219, 226, 227, 232
Moseley, Hardwick, 221
Moss, Carl (char.), 41
Mother Goddam (char.), 130
Mount Hope Cemetery (San Diego, Calif.), xv
movie industry, *see* film industry
Munro, H. H. (Saki), 11
Murder, My Sweet (film), xiii, 152–3, *152*
Murdock, Mrs. (char.), 171
Mutch, Margaret, 204
Mystery Writers of America, xv

Nabokov, Vladimir, 24
Navy Department, U.S., 144–5
Nebraska, Chandler in, 5
Neff, Walter (char.), 130–1, *130*, *134*
"Nevada Gas" (Chandler), xii, 149, 205, 210
New York, N.Y.:
  Chandler in, xv
  Cissy Pascal in, *19*
New York Times, 39
"No Crime in the Mountains" (Chandler), 46, 65, 163
Nolan, Lloyd, 152
Now, Voyager (film), 147, *148*
Nulty, Lieut. (char.), 92–3

Offord, Lenore, 139
Ohls, Bernie (char.), 49, 65, 94, 97–9
oil industry, xii, 17–18, *22*, 107
Old Forester, 54, *61*
Old Taylor, 54
O'Neill, Eugene, 35–6, *35*
Oppenheimer, Jules (char.), 139–40
Oregon, University of, 48
organized crime, 86, 87, *87*, 93–4, 98–9, 107
Ormonde, Czenzi, 158, 159
"Oscar Night in Hollywood" (Chandler), 126

Pacific Palisades, Calif., *186*
Paramount Studios, xiv, 127, *128*, *129*, 140, 144, 146, 154, 155, 156
Paris, France, Chandler in, 9–10, *9*, *10*, 13
Partridge, Eric, 206

Patton, Jim (char.), 97
"Pearls Are a Nuisance" (Chandler), xiii, 212, 217
"Pencil, The" (Chandler), 60, 65, 66, 67, 69, 88, 98–9, 122, 186–7, 211
Penn, William, 4
Pennsylvania, 4
Phyllis Dietrichson, 130–1, *130*
"Pick-Up on Noon Street" (Chandler), 109, 113
Playback (Chandler), xv, 57, 63, 64, 65, 66, 67, 82, 149
  cops in, 86
  Los Angeles in, 109
  Marlowe's instincts in, 68
  Marlowe's smoking in, 74
  Marlowe's wit in, 69, 70
  religion in, 235–7
  screenplay for, 136
  women in, 164, 166, 170, 183–4
  writing and, 208, 210, 211, 213, 214, 216
police, 85–99, *91*
Poodle Springs (Chandler), 82, 92, 186
Potter, Harlan (char.), 101, 182
Powell, Dick, 152–3, *152*
Pratt, William Henry (Boris Karloff), 9
Prendergast, Mrs. Philip Courtney (char.), 166, 174
Pride, Carol (char.), 166, 175
Prohibition, 18, 23
  organized crime and, 87, *87*
Proust, Marcel, 48
pulp magazines, 21–3, 25, 27, 46

Quakers, 4
"Qualified Farewell, A" (Chandler), 162
Quest, Orfamay (char.), 63–4, 177–8, 184

Randall, Carl (char.), 97, 176
Reavis, Lieut. (char.), 43
"Red Wind" (Chandler), xiii, 61, 113, 151, 209, 211
Regan, Vivian (char.), 41, 48, 60, 68, 79, 165, 166, 167, 172–3
Riordan, Anne (char.), 98, 175–6, 186–7
RKO, xiii, 152
Robinson, Edward G., *134*
Roman Catholics, 6
Royal Air Force, Chandler in, xi, 14–15, *14*
Russell, Leonard, 233

Saint, The (film series), 152
Saki (H. H. Munro), 11
Sam Spade, 46, *101*
Sanders, George, 152
Sanders, Sydney, 37

San Diego, Calif., Mount Hope Cemetery in, xv
Sandoe, James, 20, 35, 71, 77–8, 144–5, 189–91, 201, 219
Santa Ana winds, 112
Santa Monica, Calif., xiii, 118–19, *119*
  see also "Bay City"
Saturday Evening Post, xiii
Schwab's Pharmacy, *150*
Scripps Clinic, xv
Shakespeare, William, 34, 35, 71
Shamey, Mrs. (char.), 166
Shanghai Gesture (film), 130
Shaw, Joseph, 47
Shayne, Michael (char.), 152
Simple Art of Murder, The (Chandler), *197*
"Simple Art of Murder, The" (Chandler), xiv, 28–9, 41, 72, 77, *197*, 219, 220
slang, 205–6
"Smart-Aleck Kill" (Chandler), xii, 44, 83, 205, 209
smoking, 53–4, *54*, 73–4
"Spanish Blood" (Chandler), xii, 91, 165, 208, 212, 213, *225*
Spencer, Howard (char.), 62
Spender, Natasha, 231, *233*
Spender, Stephen, *233*
Stanwyck, Barbara, *130*
Sternwood, Carmen (char.), 172, *173*, 174
Sternwood, General (char.), 45, 215
Sternwood Mansion, *44*
Stinson, Herbert, *24*
Stoppard, Tom, 24
Stout, Rex, xviii, 221
Strangers on a Train (film), xiv, 157–61, *158*
Swanson, H. N. "Swanie," 127, 146

Taki (Chandler cat), *186*, 187–92, *188*, *190*, *191*
Taylor, Eric, *24*
This Gun for Hire (film), *141*
Thornton, Ernest, 9, 10, 13
Time, 40
Time to Kill (film), xiv, 152
To Have and Have Not (film), 153
Totter, Audrey, *50*, *155*, *169*
Trevor, Claire, *152*, *174*
Trouble Is My Business (Chandler), *xiii*, 25, 86, 91, 194, 202
"Trouble Is My Business" (Chandler), xiii, 63, 67, 165–6, 207, 208, 209, 210, 214
"Try the Girl" (Chandler), xii, 165, 166, 209, 215
Turner, Lana, *150*
"Twelve Notes on the Mystery Story" (Chandler), 194

20th Century-Fox, xiv, 146, 152
Tyndale, Jessica, 83, 123, 225, 235

Universal Pictures, 127

Van Pallandt, Nina, *182*
Vermilyea, Miss (char.), 183
Vickers, Martha, *173*
Volstead Act (1920), *87*
von Sternberg, Josef, 130

Wade, Eileen (char.), 181, *182*, 231
Wade, Roger (char.), 20, 42, 185, 197–8, 228
  Chandler's identification with, 207, 230–1
Walker, Robert, *158*
Wallace, Irving, 195, 223
Warner Bros., xiv, 127, 152, 153, 155, 157, 159
War of the Worlds, The (radio drama), *142*
Warren, Dale, 25, 33, 78, 125, 126, 134, 138, 202
Wax, John (char.), 92
Webber, Capt. (char.), 88
Weeks, Edward, 138, 204, 229
Weld, Mavis (char.), 139, 167, 168, 178, 184
Welles, Orson, *142*
Westminster Gazette, xi, 11
Whitestone, Sgt. (char.), 92
Wilde, Taggart (char.), 49

Wilder, Billy, xiv, 31, 127–30, *129*, *134*
Winslow, General (char.), 215
Wodehouse, P. G., 9
"Woman's Way, A" (Chandler), 11
World War I, Chandler and, xi, *12*, 13–15, *13*, *14*
World War II, 107–8, 144–5
"Writers in Hollywood" (Chandler), 126, 130, 136–7, 138, 139
writing, xi, 10–12, 19–40, *23*, 193–226, *196*, *197*, *199*
  animal imagery in, 212–13
  architecture in, 217–18
  education and, 201, 203
  emptiness and, 200–1
  fame and, 202–3
  literature and, 193, 198, 200, 226
  magic and, 193, 202
  mystery story form and, 218–23
  reading and, 194, 201
  routine and discipline in, 194–7
  similes and comparisons in, 206–7, 212–13, 214–17
  slang in, 205–6
  sound in, 207–8, 211–12
  style in, 203–4
  time and, 214
  wisecracks in, 49, 68–72, 214

Printed in the United States
by Baker & Taylor Publisher Services